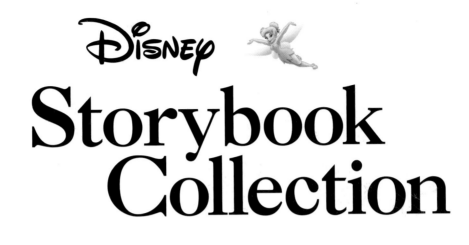

Disney
Storybook
Collection

Disney PRESS

New York

Table of Contents

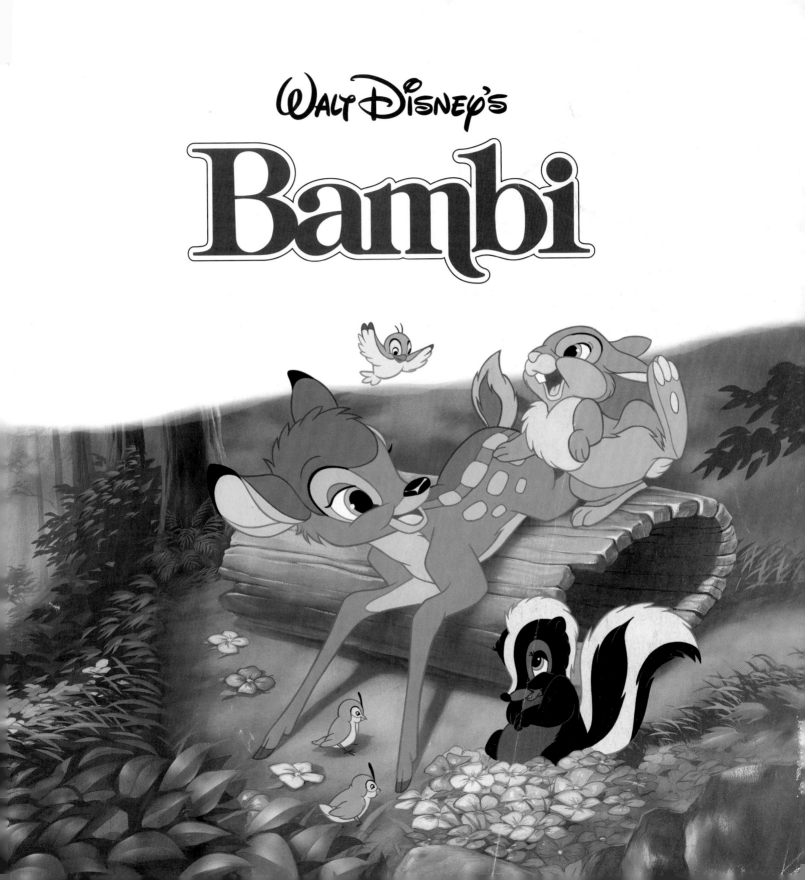

One spring morning, the animals of the forest awakened to an exciting event. Bluebirds soared through the sky chirping the news to quails, squirrels, chipmunks, and beavers.

A small bunny named Thumper heard what had happened. He hopped to see Friend Owl, who was sleeping. "Wake up!" the bunny cried and thumped his foot excitedly. "The new prince is born!"

Thumper and Friend Owl went to a small thicket. There, next to a proud doe, lay a newborn fawn. He was the new Prince of the Forest, and all the animals had come to see him.

The little prince tried to stand up. But his legs were wobbly, and he fell right back down.

Thumper giggled. "Whatcha gonna call him?" he asked.

"I think I'll call him Bambi," the mama deer said as she nuzzled her son.

Soon Bambi and his mother went for their first walk. Bambi met many of the forest animals along the way. First, Mrs. Quail and her babies stopped to say hello. Then Mrs. Opossum and her family, who liked to hang upside down from a tree, greeted him. Next, a mole poked his head out of the ground to wish Bambi a good day.

Later, Bambi tried to scamper and slipped on a reed.

"He doesn't walk very good, does he?" Thumper asked.

"What did your father tell you this morning?" Thumper's mother asked him sternly.

"If you can't say something nice," the bunny replied guiltily, "don't say nothing at all."

The bunny and his sisters ran over to help Bambi up. Then they began to play together, showing him how to hop over a log.

When they pointed out some bluebirds, Bambi tried to speak. "Bur-duh," he said slowly. With a little practice, it got easier. "Bird, bird, bird, bird!" Bambi cried.

Bambi and Thumper continued to explore the forest. A yellow butterfly landed on the fawn's tail. Bambi was fascinated with it and soon learned how to say "butterfly." When it flew to a brightly colored flower patch, Bambi and Thumper followed.

Thumper taught his new friend the word for "flower." Bambi was smelling the flowers when he found himself nose to nose with a skunk who had been doing the same thing.

"Flower!" Bambi said proudly when he saw the skunk.

Thumper laughed. "That's not a flower. He's a little—"

The skunk interrupted. "Oh, that's all right. He can call me a flower if he wants to." He giggled bashfully.

Bambi and Thumper and Flower became great friends.

One day, Bambi's mother took him to the meadow for the first time. The fawn was very excited. He hoped he might meet other deer there.

At the edge of the forest, Bambi saw the grassy meadow and bounded forward. His mother leaped in front of him.

"You must never rush out on the meadow," she warned. "The meadow is wide and open, and there are no trees or bushes to hide us, so we have to be very careful."

Once Bambi's mother told him it was safe, the young deer hurried into the soft grass, eager to play in the wide-open space. He had never been anywhere like this before.

Bambi followed a frog and came to a pond. He stopped at the water and saw his reflection. He thought it was another deer, but everywhere he moved, it moved. Finally, he realized it wasn't another deer. It was a reflection of him! Then, he saw a different image in the water and heard a giggle. A girl fawn named Faline had come to the pond. She had blue eyes and was very pretty.

As Faline got closer, Bambi ran away and hid between his mother's legs.

"He's kinda bashful, isn't he, mama?" Faline asked her mother. Faline said "hello" a couple of times and finally Bambi replied.

Soon, the two deer were frolicking in the woods. They played tag and became fast friends.

While Bambi and Faline were playing, a herd of stags galloped by. One was larger than all the rest, and the other animals in the forest stopped what they were doing to look at him.

The stag stopped for a moment and stared at Bambi. The young prince didn't know the stag was his father. "He's very brave and very wise," Bambi's mother explained to her son. "That's why he's known as the Great Prince of the Forest."

Just then, the sound of a gunshot rang out. The animals all rushed to safety. But Bambi got separated from his mother.

Luckily, the Great Prince guided him toward the thicket. Partway there, Bambi's mother joined them. When they'd made it to safety, the Great Prince left.

Time passed, and soon it was Bambi's first winter.

One day, he went to the pond with Thumper, who glided across its icy surface. "Look, the water's stiff!" Thumper exclaimed.

Bambi leaped onto the ice and fell flat on his stomach. Thumper laughed. He showed his friend how to stand up and slide across.

Winter was fun at first, but after a while Bambi longed for the warmth of spring. He was hungry, and some of his friends, including Flower, slept all winter long, and he missed them.

One afternoon, Bambi and his mother were in the forest. He was very excited because he'd found a small patch of grass. It looked like a feast. But in the distance, a shot rang out. Man was in the forest again, hunting.

He and his mother ran toward the thicket. "Faster, Bambi!" she urged. Just as he reached home, Bambi heard a second shot and noticed his mother wasn't with him anymore. He looked and looked, and then realized he was all alone.

Bambi began to cry. Soon the Great Prince came to him. "Your mother can't be with you anymore," his father said. "Man has taken her away. Now you must be brave and learn to walk alone."

Bambi lowered his head sadly.

"Come, my son," the Great Prince said. Bambi followed his father into the forest.

16

A couple of months later, spring arrived. Over the winter, Bambi had grown into a handsome young stag with antlers. His friends Thumper and Flower had grown up, too. Before long, Flower met a pretty skunk and fell in love. Then Thumper met a beautiful bunny and also fell in love.

Bambi didn't understand what had happened to his friends until he ran into Faline again. She had grown into a gorgeous doe. Bambi suddenly felt a little dizzy, but very, very happy. He and Faline were in love.

One day, a stag appeared and challenged him for Faline's love. The two deer fought. Bambi butted the stag with all his might. After a long battle, the newcomer finally limped off. Bambi had won! From that day on, he and Faline were always together.

Spring turned into summer, which faded into fall. One morning, Bambi smelled something strange—smoke. It was from a campfire. Just then a majestic stag appeared. It was Bambi's father, the Great Prince. "It's Man," he said. "We must go deep into the forest—hurry!"

Fear spread through the forest. Thumper and his family hid in their burrows. Flower and his family went underground. The beavers dove underwater, and the squirrels climbed high into the trees. Bambi and Faline ran, but soon a pack of dogs surrounded Faline. Bambi fought off the dogs, and Faline ran to safety. But a hunter shot Bambi, and he fell to the ground.

In the meantime, the forest had caught on fire. The Great Prince came and urged Bambi to get up. The young prince used all the strength he had and followed his father to an island in the river, where the rest of the animals were waiting.

They stayed there until the fire died down.

Fall once again turned into winter and winter into spring. The forest was lush and green and smelled of blooming flowers.

Soon, Thumper and his little bunnies were waking Friend Owl again. Faline had given birth to twin fawns. All the animals came to celebrate.

But no one was prouder than Bambi, the new Prince of the Forest. He stood overlooking the thicket with his father, smiling down on his family, his heart filled with love. Bambi knew he would teach his children the lessons of the forest that he had learned.

Once upon a time, there lived a lovely princess named Snow White. Her lips were red as roses and her hair was the deepest ebony. Snow White's father, the King, had died, so she lived in the castle with her stepmother, the Queen.

The Queen was very pretty, but also very cruel. She was jealous of Snow White's beauty and treated her like a servant.

Snow White was obedient and hard-working. She dreamed that someday a prince would take her away.

One afternoon, Snow White was at the well when a handsome prince *did* appear. He had heard her singing and was enchanted by her voice and her beauty. Snow White was too shy to speak to him, so she ran up to a balcony. But she could tell that the Prince was kind, and she smiled at him. He smiled back and serenaded her. On impulse, she kissed a dove and sent it to him so that he would always remember her.

The Queen had seen what had happened. She walked to her Magic Mirror. Each day, she stood in front of it and asked, "Magic Mirror on the wall, who is the fairest one of all?"

Usually the Magic Mirror told her that she was. But that day, it replied that Snow White was the fairest.

The Queen flew into a rage. She called her royal huntsman into the throne room and commanded him to take Snow White deep into the forest and kill her.

"But Your Majesty, the little princess!" he cried, shocked.

The Queen would not listen. She had made up her mind.

Soon, the huntsman took Snow White into the woods. But he could not bring himself to hurt her. "Run away, hide in the woods, anywhere. Never come back. . . ." he said.

Snow White ran and ran, but everywhere she turned, she saw something scary in the dark woods.

She fell to the ground, sobbing. A fawn walked toward her, then a chipmunk, a squirrel, and a bunny.

Snow White raised her head. "Oh!" she cried.

The animals all ran away.

"I'm awfully sorry, I didn't mean to frighten you," she said.

The animals could tell how kind Snow White was, so they walked back over to her.

"Maybe you know where I can stay?" she asked. Soon, the animals began to lead her through the woods.

At last they came to a cottage. "Oh, it's adorable," Snow White said. "Just like a dollhouse."

Snow White knocked, but no one answered the door. "Hello!" she called. "May I come in?" When no one answered, she and the animals went inside.

She noticed seven tiny chairs and a table piled high with dishes. She wondered who lived there. "Must be seven little children," she said. She looked around some more and found a shoe in a pot. Cobwebs and dust were everywhere. Then she had an idea. "I know, we'll clean the house and surprise them . . . then maybe they'll let me stay."

Snow White and the animals got to work scrubbing, sweeping, and washing.

The princess and her friends worked all day. When the downstairs was clean, she went upstairs and saw seven tiny beds with names carved in them. "Doc, Happy, Sneezy, Dopey— what funny names for children," she remarked. "Grumpy, Bashful, and Sleepy. I'm a little sleepy myself." So she lay down on the bed and took a nap.

Close by, seven little men had just left the mine where they worked. They were Dwarfs, and they lived in the cottage that Snow White had just tidied. They were glad to be going home.

When the Dwarfs reached their cottage, they noticed smoke coming from the chimney. They were worried about an intruder, so they decided to sneak inside. They opened the door quietly. No one was there, but they noticed that the whole place had been cleaned.

Just then, Happy noticed something cooking in the kettle over the fireplace. He was about to take a spoonful when Grumpy cried, "Don't touch it! It might be poison."

The Dwarfs looked around nervously. They realized the intruder must be upstairs. They sent Dopey to investigate. He went reluctantly, then ran back down. He couldn't speak, but he gestured to show the others what he had seen.

"He says it's a monster—asleep in our beds!" Doc exclaimed.

The Dwarfs grabbed their pickaxes and went upstairs. They sneaked into the bedroom and saw Snow White laying on their beds. "Why, i-i-i-i-it's a girl!" Doc cried.

"She's beautiful, just like an angel," Bashful said.

Soon, Snow White woke up. She guessed the names of all the Dwarfs—Sleepy, Grumpy, Happy, Doc, Dopey, Sneezy, and Bashful.

Snow White offered to cook and clean if she could stay with them. When the Dwarfs found out that she was a princess—and a good cook—they agreed.

After convincing them to wash up for supper, Snow White and the Dwarfs all ate together. Then they danced around the cottage and Snow White told a story. Everyone had a wonderful time—even Grumpy. Snow White was so glad to have found her new friends.

Back at the castle, the Queen consulted her Magic Mirror. But instead of telling her that she was the fairest one of all, it revealed that Snow White was still alive, and living at the Dwarfs' cottage.

The Queen knew that she had to take matters into her own hands. She decided to make a potion that would turn her into an old hag. She mixed everything together and drank it. Suddenly her hair turned white, her face became wrinkled, and her robe was transformed into rags.

She hobbled over to her book of spells and found the one she was looking for. "'One taste of the poison apple, and the victim's eyes will close forever in the sleeping death,'" she read. The only cure was Love's First Kiss. The Queen knew that once Snow White bit into the apple she would never wake up.

She dipped the apple in her cauldron and set out to find the princess.

The next morning, Snow White made the Dwarfs a hearty breakfast. Then, she gave each of them a kiss before they left for work.

The Queen soon appeared at Snow White's window dressed as the old hag. She held the poisoned apple out to Snow White. The princess's animal friends tried to warn Snow White not to take it, but she didn't understand and shooed them away. So the animals ran to the mine to get the Dwarfs.

The Queen told Snow White the apple was a magic one. "One bite and all your dreams will come true," she said.

Snow White bit into the apple after wishing that her true love would come and whisk her away to his castle. Then, she fell to the floor, as still as death.

The Dwarfs arrived at the cottage just as the Queen was leaving. They knew that she was up to no good, so they chased after her.

A thunderstorm broke out, but that didn't stop the Dwarfs. They followed the Queen into the forest and up a narrow cliff. She tried to move a huge rock so it would roll down on top of the Dwarfs and crush them.

At that moment, lightning struck. The Queen lost her balance and fell to her doom.

When the Dwarfs returned to the cottage, they found Snow White lying on the floor. She was so beautiful that they could not bring themselves to bury her. So they built a bed of gold and glass and kept watch over her day and night.

Then one day, a handsome prince rode into the forest. He was the same prince who had seen Snow White at the well. He knelt down and kissed her tenderly. Snow White's eyes fluttered open. She was awake! The Dwarfs celebrated. Then Snow White kissed them good-bye and rode off with the Prince. And they all lived happily ever after.

Everything in the animal kingdom had its place in the circle of life. When the Lion King of the Pride Lands, Mufasa, and his queen, Sarabi, had a cub named Simba, Mufasa knew that one day his son would be king. All the animals bowed in respect as the wise baboon shaman, Rafiki, introduced the young prince.

Simba grew into a healthy and energetic cub. One day, after an outing with his father, he wandered into the cave of his uncle, Scar. Until Simba was born, Mufasa's brother had been next in line for the throne. Scar was jealous of Simba, but the cub didn't know that.

Simba proudly told his uncle, "My dad just showed me the whole kingdom. And I'm gonna rule it all."

"He didn't show you what's beyond that rise at the northern border," Scar said slyly.

"He said I can't go," Simba replied.

"He's absolutely right. Only the bravest lions go there," Scar said, to tempt his nephew. "An elephant graveyard is no place for a young prince."

Simba immediately raced home and convinced Nala, a girl cub who was his best friend, to explore the Elephant Graveyard with him. When they got there, the cubs looked at the elephant bones with awe. They were just about to step inside a giant skull when Zazu, a bird who was the king's adviser, caught up to warn them how dangerous it was outside the Pride Lands.

"Danger? Ha! I walk on the wild side," Simba said confidently. "I laugh in the face of danger."

Just then, Simba turned to see three large hyenas who looked very hungry.

"Do you know what we do to kings who step out of their kingdom?" one hyena threatened.

Then the snarling hyenas chased the cubs into a ravine that was blocked by a large elephant skeleton. The cubs were trapped! Suddenly, there was a tremendous roar. Mufasa arrived and frightened the hyenas away.

Zazu took Nala home. Mufasa scolded his son for putting her in danger.

Simba was ashamed that he had disobeyed his father. "I was just trying to be brave like you," he said sadly.

"I'm only brave when I have to be," Mufasa said. "Being brave doesn't mean you go looking for trouble."

"I guess even kings get scared, huh?" Simba asked.

Mufasa nodded gravely at the young cub.

Father and son rested in the tall grass and gazed at the evening sky.

Simba loved spending time with his father. "We'll always be together, right?" he asked.

"Look at the stars," said Mufasa. "The great kings of the past look down on us from those stars. Remember that those kings will always be there to guide you. So will I."

When Scar heard that Simba had escaped, he made a plan
with the hyenas.

One day, Scar brought his nephew into a gorge and promised
him a wonderful surprise if he would wait on a certain rock.
Then on Scar's signal, the hyenas chased a herd of wildebeests
until they began a furious stampede!

As the wildebeests headed toward him, Simba climbed up a
tree. He held on tight, but he was slipping
fast. He didn't know
how much longer he
could hang on.

Suddenly, Mufasa appeared and carried Simba to a ledge. But a wildebeest slammed into Mufasa, knocking him into the thundering stampede.

"Daaaad!" Simba cried.

Mufasa leaped up and clung to the edge of a cliff, trying to pull himself to safety. By the time Simba got there, it was too late. His father had died. Simba believed Mufasa's death was his fault. He had not seen Scar push his father.

"Run away, Simba," Scar advised the young cub. "Run away and never return."

The hyenas chased the young cub far away. Then Scar returned to Pride Rock and announced to the lions that he would be their new king.

Simba ran until he collapsed in the desert from heat and exhaustion. Luckily, two curious animals found him—a meerkat called Timon and a warthog named Pumbaa.

Simba's new friends took him home to the jungle and introduced him to a new, fun-loving way of life. Timon liked to say *hakuna matata* a lot, which meant "no worries."

Even when he had his doubts, Simba tried grubs and other unusual foods that his new friends said were delicious. He played in the waterfalls and gazed at the stars with Timon and Pumbaa. It was fun, but Simba often thought about his family and his old life. He did his best to put the past behind him.

The years passed and Simba grew up. One day, a young lioness came to the jungle looking for food. Simba recognized her. It was Nala, his best friend from when he was a cub. She told him what had happened since Scar had taken over the Pride Lands. The hyenas roamed freely, and there was no food or water for anyone. Nala believed that Simba was the only one who could save them.

"We've really needed you at home," Nala said. "You're the king. If you don't do something soon, everyone will starve."

Simba was heartbroken, but he could not face going back. Then Rafiki appeared. The wise baboon convinced Simba to forget his doubts.

"You follow old Rafiki. He knows the way."

The shaman led Simba through the jungle. They stopped beside a pool of water, then Simba looked up. A vision of his father appeared in the night sky.

"You must take your place in the circle of life," Mufasa advised. "You are my son and the one true king." Simba knew his father was right.

With his friends by his side, Simba returned to Pride Rock. In front of all the animals, he confronted Scar.

"The choice is yours. Either step down or fight," Simba challenged.

Scar refused to give up his throne. Instead, he told everyone that Simba was responsible for Mufasa's death. Then he cornered his nephew on a cliff. Suddenly, Simba's foot slipped and he was hanging from the edge, just as his father had.

Scar leaned over. "Here's *my* little secret," he whispered. "I killed Mufasa."

At last Simba found the strength to fight back. He leaped up over the cliff edge and tackled his uncle. He forced Scar to admit that he was responsible for Mufasa's death. Hearing the truth, the lion pride defended Simba against the hyenas.

Simba and Scar battled across Pride Rock, exchanging powerful blows. Finally, they both fell near the edge. Simba ordered his uncle to leave the Pride Lands. But Scar attacked Simba again. Simba dodged the blow and Scar fell over the side of the cliff.

When the fighting was over, Simba took his rightful place as the Lion King and restored the Pride Lands to a place of peace and beauty. Simba and Nala found happiness together, and when their little cub was born, a new circle of life began.

On a quiet street in London lived a family named the Darlings. Mr. and Mrs. Darling had three children—Wendy, John, and Michael. All three played and slept in the nursery.

Wendy was the oldest. Each night before bed, she told her brothers all about the adventures of a hero named Peter Pan.

John and Michael loved those stories. They romped through the house, pretending to have sword fights with pirates and look for treasure, just like Peter Pan.

One night, Mr. Darling was getting ready to go out with his wife. He was quite frantic because his gold cuff links were missing, and Michael had drawn a treasure map on his last clean shirt. Mr. Darling blamed Wendy for filling the boys' heads with stories of Peter Pan.

He decided that night would be Wendy's last in the nursery. He thought she was ready to have a room of her own. Wendy was shocked. The boys were, too.

"Sooner or later, people have to grow up," Mr. Darling said.

Mrs. Darling tucked the children in, and before long, they were fast asleep.

Later that night, Peter Pan and a fairy named Tinker Bell flew into the nursery. Peter often listened outside the window while Wendy told stories about him. The last time he was there, he'd lost his shadow and he needed it back.

Soon, he found the shadow, but it tried to escape. Luckily, Wendy woke up and insisted upon sewing it back on. She told Peter that it was her last night in the nursery, for tomorrow she would have to grow up.

"No, I won't have it!" cried Peter. "Come on!"

"But where are we going?" asked Wendy.

"Never Land," he replied. "You'll never grow up there."

With all the commotion, John and Michael woke up. Peter Pan agreed that they could come along, too.

After a sprinkling of pixie dust, the Darling children rose into the air and followed Peter and Tinker Bell out the window. "We can fly!" they shouted as they flew over the city.

Meanwhile, back in Never Land, a pirate named Captain Hook was busy scheming with his first mate, Mr. Smee. Hook wanted revenge against Peter Pan. Long ago, Peter had chopped off Hook's hand in a sword fight and thrown it to a crocodile to eat. The Crocodile thought it was delicious and now he followed the pirate everywhere, hoping for another bite. Hook was constantly on the lookout for the hungry animal.

Hook didn't know where to find Peter, so he decided to kidnap Tiger Lily, the Indian Chief's daughter. She was a good friend of Peter Pan's, and Hook was sure they could get her to reveal the location of his hideout.

As Peter, Tinker Bell, and the children approached Never Land, Peter shouted, "There it is, Wendy!" and pointed to the wondrous land below.

"Oh, Peter, it's just as I've always dreamed it would be!" Wendy replied excitedly.

But Captain Hook had spotted Peter Pan flying in the clouds.

He shot a cannonball toward them. Peter and the children jumped behind a cloud. Luckily, it zoomed by and they didn't get hurt.

"Quick, Tink! Take Wendy and the boys to the island!" yelled Peter as he raced down toward Hook's ship.

While Peter distracted Hook, Tinker Bell hurried toward the island. She flew so fast that Wendy, John, and Michael fell far behind. The fairy thought Peter Pan was spending too much time with Wendy. She was jealous, so she went to see the Lost Boys, who lived with Peter in Hangman's Tree. Peter was their leader—they'd do anything he said. So Tink told them that he wanted them to shoot the Wendy bird out of the sky.

The Lost Boys grabbed their slingshots and aimed at Wendy. Fortunately, Peter arrived in time to save her as she fell toward the ground. He was very angry with Tinker Bell, though.

"Tinker Bell, I hereby banish you forever!" he shouted.

"Please, not forever," Wendy pleaded. She and her brothers were fine, after all.

"Well, for a week then," Peter agreed. But Tink didn't hear him. She had already flown away.

Next, Peter took Wendy on a tour of Never Land. While visiting the mermaids, Peter spotted Hook interrogating Tiger Lily, who was tied to a rock in the water. The pirate was still convinced she knew the location of Peter's hiding place. But Tiger Lily wouldn't give him any information.

Peter revealed himself and challenged Hook. They fought one another, and as they did, the rising tide got closer and closer to Tiger Lily's head. Peter Pan finally won, sending Hook into the water, where the Crocodile was waiting. The pirate swam away quickly, and Smee rowed out to save him.

Peter swooped down and rescued Tiger Lily just as the water was about to cover her. He brought her safely back to her village. Her father, the Chief, named Peter "Eagle Feathers," and there was a great celebration.

The only one who didn't celebrate was Tinker Bell. She still thought Peter had banished her forever and was very upset. Captain Hook had heard what had happened and he sent Smee to fetch her immediately. Hook persuaded Tink to tell him that Hangman's Tree was the entrance to Peter's hiding place. But before she did, she made him promise not to harm Peter Pan.

Later, while Peter was out, Hook's pirates went to his hideout and kidnapped Wendy, John, Michael, and the Lost Boys. Hook left a bomb (disguised as a present!) for Peter. Then he took the children back to his ship and tied them up. They didn't know how they would ever escape.

Tinker Bell was shocked when she discovered Hook's plans to blow up Peter. With only minutes to spare, she flew as fast as she could to warn him. Peter was about to unwrap the present, but Tink grabbed it right before it exploded. *Kaboom!*

Peter didn't think Tinker Bell had survived the blast. He was upset, but he didn't want anyone else to get hurt, so he raced back to Hook's ship to save the children. When he got there, Wendy was walking the plank! Peter caught her right before she fell in the water.

Then he jumped on the ship's deck and challenged Hook. "This time you've gone too far!" he yelled. Just then, Tinker Bell flew by. She had survived!

"You wouldn't dare fight old Hook man-to-man," the pirate sneered.

"I'll fight you man-to-man with one hand behind my back!" countered Peter.

They began to duel.

Meanwhile, John, Michael, and the Lost Boys climbed to the crow's nest and battled the other pirates. The Lost Boys threw rocks and fired slingshots just as the pirates got close to them. John even hit them on the head with his umbrella. One by one, the pirates were defeated—all except Hook, who was still fighting Peter.

Peter and Hook battled it out on the ship's yardarm, which had swung over the water. Peter grabbed Hook's sword, but then decided to let him go. But the pirate had been humiliated. He took a swipe at Peter, lost his balance, and plunged into the water—right into the jaws of the Crocodile.

"Smee!" Hook cried as the ferocious Crocodile chased him far out to sea.

"Cap'n, wait for us!" his first mate yelled as he and the pirates rowed after Hook in a small lifeboat.

Peter took control of Hook's ship, and Wendy and the rest of the children cheered. "Hooray for Captain Pan!"

"Could you tell me, sir, where we're sailing?" asked Wendy with a smile.

"To London, Madam," replied Peter.

"Michael, John . . . we're going home!" cried Wendy joyfully. The children were all very happy for they had gotten homesick.

Tinker Bell sprinkled the ship with pixie dust, and soon it was flying out of the water, through the air, and back to London. Below them, Never Land grew smaller and smaller until it finally disappeared. Wendy and her brothers said good-bye to Peter. They knew they would always remember their marvelous adventure.

At home, Wendy told her parents she was ready to grow up. Then they gazed out the window together, just in time to see the ship pass across the moon.

"You know," Mr. Darling said, his arm around his daughter, "I have the strangest feeling that I've seen that ship before . . . a long time ago."

THREE LITTLE PIGS

Once upon a time, there were three little pigs. The pigs were brothers who had been living in the same house. They decided they were old enough to build homes of their own. They set off down the road.

The first little pig did not like to work at all. He soon found a spot for his house. He decided to build it out of straw because that was the fastest way. When he was done, he danced down the road to see how his brothers' houses were coming along.

The second little pig did not like to work either, so he decided to make his house out of sticks. It would be quick and easy. Before long, he was finished. His house was not very strong, but at least his work was done.

The first little pig played the flute while his brother played the fiddle and danced. After a while, the two pigs went down the road to see their other brother.

The third little pig was the serious one. He wanted his house to be strong and did not mind working hard. For he knew that in the nearby woods there lived a big, bad wolf who liked nothing better than to catch little pigs and eat them! So he built his house out of bricks. He worked and worked, putting each and every brick carefully in place.

The first two pigs laughed when they saw their brother hard at work. But the third little pig just ignored them and continued to build his house. "You can laugh and dance and sing!" he called after his brothers as they went back to their houses. "But I'll be safe and you'll be sorry when the wolf comes to the door!"

The first pig was sitting inside his house of straw when the wolf came knocking at the door.

"Little pig, little pig, let me come in!" cried the wolf.

"Not by the hair of my chinny-chin-chin!" shouted the little pig.

"Then I'll huff and I'll puff and I'll blow your house in!" roared the wolf.

He took a deep breath and blew the straw house down! Not one piece was left standing.

The poor little pig ran down the road to his brother's house. Soon after he got to the house of sticks, the wolf knocked on the door. He knew that the pigs would not let him in, so he disguised himself as a sheep.

Luckily, the two pigs could tell it was the wolf. "You can't fool us with that sheepskin!" they cried.

"Then I'll huff and I'll puff and I'll blow your house in!" yelled the wolf.

And he blew the little house of twigs all to pieces!

77

The two pigs raced off to their brother's brick house and hid under the bed.

"Don't worry," the third little pig said to his brothers. "You are safe here."

Soon, they were laughing and playing music.

The wolf could hear the little pigs having fun inside. So he decided to blow the house down. Then the pigs would have nowhere to run and hide. He huffed and he puffed and he puffed and he huffed. But no matter how hard he tried, he could not blow down that little house of bricks.

The wolf thought and thought about how he could get inside. Then he realized he could climb down the chimney. And so he did. But the three little pigs were ready for him—a kettle of boiling water was hanging in the fireplace.

"*Yeeoowwww!!!*" the wolf yelled as he fell into the hot water. He flew straight up the chimney and ran into the woods. The three little pigs never saw him again.

The next day, the three pigs went to work again. They built two more brick houses, so each little pig would have a nice, strong house of his own.

Long ago, in ancient Greece, powerful gods battled against monstrous creatures called Titans. The Titans loved to make trouble. They caused huge earthquakes and giant tidal waves. So Zeus, king of the gods, zapped them with mighty thunderbolts and locked them away. Peace was restored, and from high atop Mount Olympus, the gods ruled the world.

Many years later, Zeus's wife, the goddess Hera, gave birth to a baby boy named Hercules. Zeus was very happy and very proud—his son was strong, just like him.

To celebrate Hercules's birth, all the gods gathered around to see the baby and give him gifts. Zeus made a special gift for his son out of clouds—a winged horse named Pegasus.

But not everyone was happy for Zeus. There was one god who did not like him at all. He was Hades, lord of the Underworld.

Hades decided that he would take over Olympus and make Zeus his prisoner. When the time was right, he would unleash the Titans.

To find out if his strategy would work, Hades went to see the Fates. The Fates were three sisters who shared one eye and could see into the future. They told Hades that he would defeat Zeus in eighteen years, when the planets lined up. "The once proud Zeus will finally fall, and you, Hades, will rule them all," the Fates chanted. There was just one catch—if Hercules fought against the Titans, Hades's plan would fail.

Hades decided to get rid of little Hercules. The lord of the Underworld sent his henchmen, Pain and Panic, to steal the baby and feed him a potion that would make him human.

Pain and Panic went to Mount Olympus and snuck into Hercules's room. They grabbed the baby and took him down to Earth, where they started to feed him the potion. After a while, they were interrupted by a kindly older couple named Amphitryon and Alcmene.

Pain and Panic ran away and left Hercules behind. The couple decided to adopt the baby. When they saw the gold medallion of the gods around his neck, they knew Hercules was not a normal boy. Because he hadn't finished the potion, Hercules was still as strong as a god, but now he was human.

As Hercules grew into a teenager, he was strong, but he was also clumsy. He did his best to fit in, but something always happened to make him stand out. When he tried to play a simple game of catch, he knocked over the stone pillars in the marketplace! Hercules knew he didn't belong.

Seeing how sad he was, Amphitryon and Alcmene told their adopted son about his past and the medallion they had found around his neck.

"Maybe the gods will have the answers," Hercules said when he saw the medallion. He decided to go to a temple and find out.

In the temple, Hercules called out to the statue of Zeus and demanded to know the truth. With a mighty bolt of lightning, the statue came alive.

"Is this the greeting you give your father?" Zeus asked. Then he explained that Hercules was his son. He said that if Hercules could prove himself to be a true hero on Earth, he could return to Mount Olympus.

Zeus told Hercules to go and find Philoctetes, who would help train him. As the young man turned to go, Zeus let out a

loud whistle. Suddenly, Pegasus appeared. The winged horse was all grown up. Hercules hopped on the horse's back and set out to find the famous Philoctetes.

Philoctetes, or Phil, agreed to train him. He made Hercules
practice rescues and learn to control his strength. After a lot of
training, Phil thought the young man was ready to be tested,
so they went to the city of Thebes. On the way, Hercules saw
a woman being chased by a centaur—a beast that was half
man and half horse. This was his chance to be a hero! He
battled the centaur and won.

At the battle, a woman named
Megara saw what Hercules
had done and was impressed.
"My friends call
me Meg," she told him.
Hercules fell instantly
in love. But there was
something he didn't know:
Meg worked for Hades.

Hades had been keeping an eye on Hercules. The young man had been saving people all over ancient Greece and had never gotten hurt. Hades needed to get Hercules out of the way, so he forced him to battle the Hydra—another frightening monster. The Hydra was fierce and dangerous, but it was no match for Hercules.

Hades was furious, so he sent Meg to find Hercules's weakness. Meg and Hercules spent a wonderful afternoon together. "Until I met you," Hercules told Meg, "I felt so alone." They hugged.

Hades realized the two were in love and saw his chance. He went to Hercules and told him that unless he gave up his strength for twenty-four hours, Meg would get hurt. Hercules didn't want anything to happen to Meg, so he agreed.

Now that Hercules was out of the way, it was time to unleash the Titans from their prison. With a zap, Hades sent all but one after Zeus. He saved the one-eyed Cyclops for Hercules.

The Cyclops headed for Thebes to destroy Hercules and the city. Hercules was weak and could not fight the one-eyed beast. The Cyclops quickly bruised and battered the young man. Just when he was about to give up, Hercules saw a burning tree branch. He used it to blind the Cyclops, who fell into the sea. Hercules had won again—this time by using his head.

As Hercules celebrated his victory, a damaged column started to fall. Meg, who had come to find Hercules, pushed the hero out of the way. The pillar fell on her with a loud crash.

Because Meg had been hurt, that meant Hercules got his strength back. Leaving Meg with Phil, Hercules headed for Mount Olympus to stop Hades and the Titans. He managed to defeat the Titans, but in the meantime, Hades found Meg and threw her into the Pit of Souls. Hercules knew he had to save her. Hades watched gleefully as the hero dived into the Pit of Souls. No mortal had ever made it out alive. As Hercules swam after Meg, he began to grow older and weaker—before long, he was near death.

With his last bit of strength, Hercules rescued Meg. He had proven he was a true hero. Now he could go home to Mount Olympus. But instead, Hercules decided to stay on Earth. He belonged with Meg, after all.

Once upon a time, there was a prince who was very handsome, but also selfish and unkind. One cold winter's night, a poor old woman went to his castle and asked if she could stay there. The cruel prince refused. Then the woman revealed that she was an enchantress.

As punishment for his behavior, she put the prince and all who lived in his castle under a powerful spell.

The prince was turned into a terrible beast, and all of his servants were changed into enchanted household objects.

Mrs. Potts, the cook, and her son, Chip, became a teapot and teacup. Cogsworth, the head butler, became a mantel clock. And Lumiere, the maître d', became a candelabrum.

According to the spell, the prince and all his servants would change back into humans only if the prince learned to love someone and be loved by his twenty-first birthday. Because he was so ashamed of his hideous appearance, the Beast kept himself hidden in his castle. He could only see the outside world through a magical mirror.

Not far from the castle there lived a lovely young woman named Belle. She longed for a life of excitement and adventure, but in her small village the only adventure to be found was in the books she loved to read.

Gaston, a hunter who lived in the same village, had no interest at all in books. But he *was* interested in Belle. "She's the lucky girl I'm going to marry," he bragged to his friends. Belle, on the other hand, thought Gaston was a bully who was only interested in himself. She had no intention of marrying him.

One dark winter day, Belle's father, Maurice, started out on a journey. On his way through the forest, he and his horse, Philippe, got lost. As night fell, Maurice sought shelter in a gloomy castle—the same castle where the Beast lived!

Maurice was greeted by the Beast's servants, Cogsworth and Lumiere. They were glad to have company and eagerly welcomed him.

Maurice was quite surprised that the servants were enchanted household objects, but he was happy to have a warm place to stay.

Cogsworth was worried about what would happen if his master saw their unexpected guest. The Beast was very ferocious and didn't like anyone from the outside world to see him.

When the Beast discovered that Maurice was in the castle, he roared, "You are not welcome here!" He believed that Maurice had come to make fun of his terrible appearance, and so he dragged him off to the dungeon!

Maurice was very frightened.

The next morning, Maurice's horse arrived at home alone. Belle knew something had gone terribly wrong. "Where's Papa?" she cried. "Take me to him!" She climbed on Philippe's back and rode all the way to the Beast's castle.

Belle bravely went through the gate and into the castle, but her courage was not to be rewarded. The Beast refused to release Maurice. "There's nothing you can do," said the Beast. "He's my prisoner." Only when Belle offered to take her father's place— forever—did the Beast finally agree to let him go.

Maurice went back to the village to round up some help. "I need your help! He's got her locked in the dungeon!" he cried.

"Slow down, Maurice. Who's got Belle locked in a dungeon?" asked Gaston.

"A beast! A horrible monstrous beast!" replied Maurice.

Gaston began to plot his next move. He would rescue Belle and convince her to marry him.

At the castle, the Beast's enchanted servants tried to make Belle feel at home. Cogsworth, Lumiere, Mrs. Potts, and little Chip knew that if Belle and the Beast fell in love, the spell over the castle would be broken. The Beast didn't think that someone as beautiful as Belle would ever fall in love with him, but the servants were hopeful.

The servants even hosted an amazing dinner just for Belle, complete with music and candlelight. The forks, spoons, napkins, and plates all danced together. They thought that maybe if Belle grew to like the castle, she would grow to like their master as well.

From the very beginning of Belle's time at the
castle, the Beast was kinder to her than
he had been to her father. He allowed
her to live in a room, instead of the
dungeon. He rescued her from
wolves that attacked her when
she tried to run away. When
the Beast got hurt fighting the

wolves, Belle helped him back to the castle and bandaged him.
The Beast was touched by her kindness. One day, he decided to do
something special for her. "Belle," he said, "there's something I want
to show you. But first you have to close your eyes. It's a surprise."

He led her into a room and asked her to open her eyes.

In front of Belle was the most magnificent library she had ever
seen. "I've never seen so many books!" she exclaimed.

"It's yours," said the Beast.

Each day, the Beast tried his hardest to be pleasant. Belle slowly grew fonder of him. One night, they had a romantic dinner together. The Beast dressed in a dashing blue coat, and Belle wore a golden gown. They talked and laughed. Then he whirled her around the ballroom floor in a beautiful dance.

But Belle's heart still ached for her father. "If only I could see him again," she told the Beast.

"There is a way," he replied. He handed her a small mirror. "This mirror will show you anything—anything you wish to see."

Belle asked to see her father. Maurice appeared in the mirror, looking tired and sick. "He may be dying, and he's all alone," she told the Beast sadly.

"Then you must go to him!" urged the Beast. He loved Belle too much to keep her away from her father—even if she was his only hope to break the spell.

Belle returned to her village and nursed her father back to health. She told everyone how kind the Beast had been. Gaston became very angry. He got ahold of the magic mirror that the Beast had given Belle and convinced the villagers that the Beast was dangerous and should be destroyed. Then he led an angry mob to the castle.

Mrs. Potts tried to warn the Beast that his castle was under attack, but after Belle left he had lost all desire to go on. "It doesn't matter now," he said. "Just let them come."

But the Beast's servants weren't going to give up that easily. With all their might, they fought back against the mob of townspeople. When they had finally driven the mob away, the servants cheered. They had won!

Gaston, however, was still on the grounds. He found the Beast and attacked. Soon the two of them were fighting on the castle rooftop. Midway through the battle, the Beast heard Belle's voice in the distance. She had come back! With new determination, he grabbed Gaston's club, and the two struggled. In a last attempt to kill the Beast, Gaston lost his footing and fell to his death. The fight was finally over.

Belle rushed to the Beast's side. He was badly wounded. "You came back," he whispered.

Belle's tears fell upon the Beast. "Of course I came back!" she cried. "I love you!"

With those magical words, the spell was broken! The Beast was transformed into a handsome prince, and the enchanted servants became human once more.

"It's a miracle!" declared Lumiere.

At last, Belle had found what she had always longed for: a life full of excitement, romance, and adventure. And she and her prince lived happily ever after.

Walt Disney's
Mickey and the Beanstalk

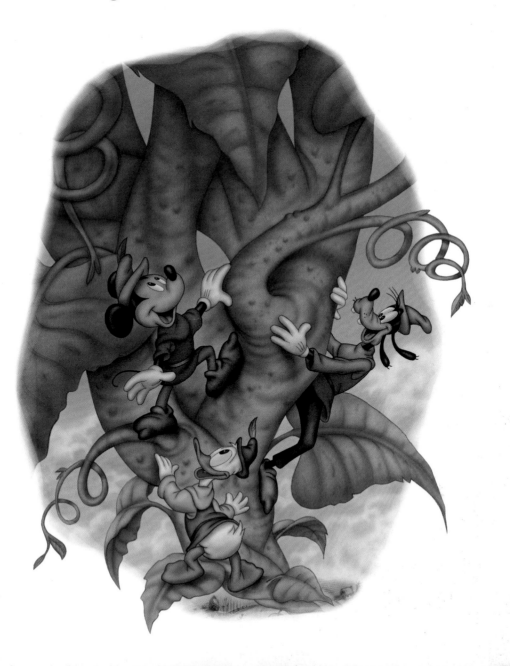

Long, long ago, there was a place where the sun shone every day. It was called Happy Valley. Everything there was pretty and green and . . . happy.

High on a hilltop overlooking the valley stood a castle. Inside were many beautiful things, but the most beautiful thing of all was a golden harp. It was no ordinary harp, though. This harp sang sweetly and had the face of an angel. Its magical music cast a spell of peace over Happy Valley.

But one day, a mysterious shadow darkened the whole valley. When it went away, the harp had disappeared. No one knew where it had gone.

Without the harp, the magic spell was broken. Slowly, everything stopped working and growing. Soon, there was nothing to eat, and the people grew sad and hungry.

Three farmers were sadder and hungrier than anyone else—Farmer Mickey, Farmer Donald, and Farmer Goofy. They only had a slice of bread and a few beans between them. They decided there was nothing left to do but sell their cow, Bossy, in exchange for food.

When Mickey returned from selling Bossy, he showed Donald and Goofy what he had been paid.

"Three beans!" his friends cried angrily when Mickey held out his hand. "We can't live on three beans!" Donald grabbed the beans and threw them on the floor.

"But they are magic beans," Mickey tried to explain as he watched the beans roll through a hole. No one believed him. That night, the three farmers went to bed hungrier than ever. They didn't know what they would do.

Then, under the bright moonlight, something strange happened. The beans began to grow. A stem formed and quickly turned into a huge stalk that climbed all the way to the sky, carrying the farmers' little house with it.

When the hungry farmers awoke, they looked out the window. Happy Valley was gone! They were in a strange land on top of the clouds. All they could see was a very big castle.

"Let's go!" cried Mickey. "Whoever lives there must have plenty of food. Maybe he'll share!"

The three friends ran to the castle. They scaled giant steps and then slid under a massive door. When they finally got inside, they spotted huge bowls and plates filled with food.

The farmers ran to the table and started eating everything in sight, from cheese to potatoes. It was like a dream come true!

116

Just as they finished, they heard a tiny voice call out to them from a small trunk on the table.

"Who are you?" Mickey asked as he looked in the keyhole.

"It is I, the golden harp," said the tiny voice. "A wicked giant stole me and brought me here to sing for him. The sound helps him sleep."

The farmers were very frightened when they heard the word "giant." They were definitely *not* giants.

Just then, everything in the room started shaking, and heavy footsteps thundered down the long, dark hall. A voice roared out, "Fee-fi-fo-fum!"

Mickey, Donald, and Goofy hid on the table behind a bowl, a salt shaker, and a pitcher. The giant entered the room—he was taller than ten men and looked stronger than forty!

The giant walked to the table and started to make himself a big meal. As he reached for various foods, the three friends had to pick new hiding spots. Mickey hid in the bread. But the giant used the bread to make a sandwich and Mickey got stuck inside! The giant was about to take a bite when he noticed the farmer wriggling around.

"Gotcha!" the giant cried, grabbing Mickey. Then he scooped up Donald and Goofy from their hiding spots and dropped all three into the box where the golden harp was kept. But Mickey managed to escape.

The giant grabbed the harp, locked the box, and slipped the key into his pocket. He did not know Mickey was free.

The giant walked to a nearby chair and placed the harp on the table in front of him. The harp sang sweetly and lulled the giant to sleep.

When Mickey heard the giant snoring, he climbed down a piece of thread. Then, ever so carefully, he reached into the giant's pocket and took the key.

As quickly as he could, Mickey let his friends out of the box and grabbed the harp. But as they made their way to the front door, the giant opened one eye!

"Come back here!" he roared.

Carrying the harp, the farmers raced to the beanstalk and slid down toward the valley below. When they reached the ground, Donald and Goofy grabbed a saw and began to cut down the beanstalk.

But the giant had followed them and was climbing down, down, down. Donald and Goofy kept sawing. At last, the beanstalk began to wobble, and then, it toppled over. Then the giant crashed to the ground and was still.

The farmers took the golden harp back to the castle on the hilltop, where she could sing again. Happy Valley was a very cheerful place once more. And no one was more pleased than the three brave friends—Farmer Mickey, Farmer Donald, and Farmer Goofy. They had saved the harp *and* Happy Valley!

Disney's
The Aristocats

Long ago, a kindly old woman named Madame Bonfamille lived in a beautiful house in Paris. She had a cat named Duchess, who had three kittens named Toulouse, Berlioz, and Marie. The kittens were very talented. Toulouse could paint, and Berlioz could play the piano. Marie, who had white fur like her mother, liked to sing.

Madame loved Duchess and her kittens very much. She even made plans to leave her entire fortune to them. But when her butler, Edgar, found out, he was very upset. He had been taking care of Madame and her cats for years and had always thought he would inherit her fortune. Edgar decided to make the cats disappear, so Madame would leave her money to him instead.

That evening, Edgar put something in the cats' supper that would make them very sleepy.

"Come taste this delicious crème de la crème à la Edgar!" he called as he set down their food.

The cats and their mouse friend Roquefort ate it all up. Roquefort went to his mouse hole to rest, and the cats fell asleep.

Edgar put the cats in a basket and drove them out to the country. Along the way, two noisy dogs started to chase them. Edgar lost control of his motorcycle and drove into a river.

The basket holding the cats fell off the motorcycle and rolled under a bridge. Edgar couldn't find it, so he returned to Paris. When he got home, Roquefort had awakened. The mouse began to suspect that Edgar was behind the cats' disappearance.

When Duchess and her kittens
woke up, they were in the dark
countryside. They didn't know how
they had gotten there or how to
get home. It was raining, so they
huddled together to stay warm.

Luckily, the next morning, an alley
cat named Thomas O'Malley found the kittens
and their mother at the bridge. He knew the journey back to
Paris would be difficult for the little ones, so he offered to help.

O'Malley snuck the family onto a milk truck. As the truck
began to move, Marie fell off the back. The alley cat rescued her

and hopped aboard. The cats drank
some of the cream on the truck, but
when the driver discovered them, he
chased them away.

After a very long walk, a bridge crossing, and an accidental tumble into a river, the cats finally reached Paris late at night. O'Malley had stayed with Duchess and her kittens the entire time.

Berlioz, Toulouse, and Marie were very tired from the journey. O'Malley decided they needed a rest before they went home. He led them across the rooftops to his house.

When they got to O'Malley's place, some of his friends were there singing and playing jazz. The leader of the jazz band stepped forward, and O'Malley introduced him as Scat Cat. He was the coolest cat on the Parisian jazz scene, and he could play the trumpet and sing better than anyone.

The cats had never heard jazz before, but soon all the kittens were dancing. Then O'Malley asked Duchess to dance. The band played one jazz tune after another, and before long it was very late.

The kittens were still humming when their mother put them to bed. They had never had so much fun.

Then O'Malley
and Duchess
went out to the
roof and looked
at the starry sky.
They'd had a
wonderful evening
together. O'Malley
knew he was in love
with Duchess, and he
asked her to stay.

"Oh, Thomas, that would be
wonderful," she said. Duchess loved O'Malley very much and
knew her kittens did, too, but she also knew she could never
leave Madame.

"You're just her house pets," O'Malley protested.

"Oh, no," Duchess said. "We mean far more to her than that."

"I'm gonna miss you . . ." O'Malley said. "And those kids."

The next day, O'Malley reluctantly took his new friends home. At the front door, they said their good-byes and Duchess and the kittens went inside.

Edgar was mad that the cats had returned, so he put them inside a sack and hid them inside a huge trunk to be sent far away to Timbuktu.

But Roquefort had been keeping an eye on Edgar. When he saw what had happened, he ran down the street to catch up with O'Malley. Luckily, the cat hadn't gotten too far.

"Duchess . . . kittens . . . in trouble!" cried the little mouse. O'Malley stopped and listened, then came up with a plan to help the cats.

135

O'Malley sent Roquefort to get Scat Cat and his friends and bring them to Madame's. Then he ran into the house to help Duchess. He chased Edgar into the barn and cornered him. O'Malley jumped on the butler's back, but Edgar shook the cat off. When O'Malley tried to get to the trunk to free the cats, Edgar fought him with a pitchfork!

Suddenly, Scat Cat and the gang were at the barn door. They managed to overpower the butler. Roquefort opened the trunk, and O'Malley let the cats out. Then they made Edgar get into the trunk. A few minutes later, some men came to pick it up. Finally, Edgar was gone—headed for Timbuktu.

Duchess and the kittens had a joyful reunion with Madame. She was delighted her precious pets were safely home and very grateful to Thomas O'Malley and his friends.

Madame could see that O'Malley and Duchess were in love, so she invited the alley cat to live with them. Duchess and the kittens were very happy, because now their family was complete.

Once upon a time, a mermaid named Ariel disobeyed her father's orders and ventured into the world above the ocean's surface. There she saw a human celebrating his birthday aboard a festive sailing ship. His friends called him Prince Eric. Ariel thought he was very handsome and wished she could meet him.

Suddenly, a hurricane swept in. The storm tore the ship apart and threw its passengers into the sea. Ariel dived after the young prince to rescue him from the threatening waves.

She found Prince Eric and dragged him to the shore. As the prince lay unconscious, she touched his face tenderly and sang to him. When she heard someone call his name, she quickly returned to the sea and watched from afar as one of his servants discovered him. She wished that she could have remained on the beach with him.

The next day, the royal court composer, Sebastian the crab, went to see Ariel. He was a trusted friend of her father, King Triton. Sebastian tried to convince Ariel that she had a good life as a mermaid. "Life under the sea is better than anything up there," he told her. But nothing he said could change her mind. Ariel was in love.

Only Flounder, a fish who was Ariel's most loyal friend, understood. He had noticed that a statue of the prince had landed in Ariel's secret grotto after the shipwreck. The grotto was where she kept human-made objects that she had found. He led Ariel to the sculpture, knowing she'd be thrilled.

"Flounder, you're the best!" she cried, when she saw it. "It looks just like him."

Just then, King Triton appeared. He knew that Ariel had made contact with the human world. He was worried because she could have been hurt, and furious because she had disobeyed him.

Ariel told her father about Prince Eric. "Daddy, I love him!" she cried.

But the little mermaid couldn't convince her father that she was meant to be with the prince. In a final attempt to protect her from the dangers of the human world, King Triton raised his trident and destroyed all of Ariel's human-made treasures— even the statue.

Ariel was determined to find a way to be with Eric. But she knew her father would never help her. So she went to the evil sea witch, Ursula, and they made a deal. In exchange for Ariel's beautiful voice, Ursula transformed the mermaid's tail into legs. Ariel would remain human only if she received the kiss of true love before sunset on the third day. If she didn't, she'd turn back into a mermaid and would become Ursula's servant forever.

Ariel swam to the surface with her new legs. Happy to be
human at last, she wiggled her toes excitedly while Sebastian
watched in shock. "I'm gonna march myself home right now and
tell the sea king!" he cried. But when he looked at the sadness in
Ariel's eyes, he knew that she would never be happy as a mermaid.
"All right," he decided, "I'll help you find your prince."

Scuttle, Ariel's seagull friend, happily made her a dress out of
a ship's sail and a rope. It wasn't long before Prince Eric arrived
on the beach.

"You're the one!" Eric exclaimed when he saw her. "The one I have been looking for!" Ariel nodded enthusiastically. Then, Eric remembered that the girl who had rescued him had a beautiful voice. But Ariel wasn't able to speak. "Oh, you couldn't be who I thought," he said with a sigh.

Still, he helped her to the castle. When they ate dinner together that night, Ariel used a fork to comb her hair and made Eric laugh for the first time in weeks.

The next day, the prince took Ariel on a tour of his kingdom. She was fascinated with everything from horses to puppet shows. They danced in the marketplace, and Ariel even drove the carriage on the ride back. Eric was delighted by his new guest and pleased with her fun-loving nature.

Ariel enjoyed the day, too. But the two still hadn't kissed. Would she be able to make him fall in love with her in time?

That evening, Ariel and Eric rowed together in a quiet lagoon. Soon the prince found himself leaning close to Ariel.

Just when he was about to kiss her, Ursula's pet eels showed up and tipped the boat over! Eric helped Ariel swim ashore.

Deep under the sea, Ursula watched through a crystal ball. She was determined to do everything in her power to make sure there was no kiss. Then she transformed herself into a beautiful woman named Vanessa. That night, she arrived at Eric's castle and hypnotized the prince. She used Ariel's voice, which was trapped in a seashell necklace, to make Eric believe that she was the girl who had rescued him. When Ariel awakened, Vanessa had already planned a wedding.

The ceremony was to take place aboard a boat. Scuttle gathered all the sea creatures he could find to help him delay it, while Flounder helped Ariel swim to the ship. Scuttle managed to pull the magic seashell necklace from Vanessa's neck, and Ariel got her voice back.

Once the spell on Prince Eric was broken, he realized that Ariel was his true love. But just as he was about to kiss her, she became a mermaid again. Then Vanessa turned back into Ursula.

Ursula pulled Ariel into the water. But Eric wouldn't give her up without a fight.

"I lost her once. I'm not going to lose her again!" the prince yelled as he maneuvered a rowboat across the ocean. He shot a harpoon at the sea witch, but her pet eels dragged him below the waves.

Ursula grew to a monstrous size, towering above them all. She used the sea king's trident to create a whirlpool, which caused Eric's old ship to be lifted up from the ocean floor. The prince climbed aboard the vessel and steered it directly toward the powerful sea witch. He hit her head on. She sank into the ocean—gone forever.

Eric jumped from the ship and swam to safety. As he lay exhausted on the shore, Ariel watched from a rock far out in the water.

Turning to Sebastian, King Triton said, "She really does love him, doesn't she?" He granted his beautiful daughter her greatest wish—to become part of the human world—and watched happily as she married her prince. Then Ariel and Eric sailed toward their kingdom, where they lived happily ever after.

THE JUNGLE BOOK

Long ago, deep in the jungles of India, there lived a wise black panther named Bagheera. One day, as Bagheera walked along the river, he saw something surprising—a baby! It was lying in a boat that had crashed onto shore. "Why, it's a Man-cub!" the panther said to himself.

Bagheera took the child to the den of a nearby wolf family. The mother had just had pups, and Bagheera hoped she would take care of the Man-cub. The panther placed the baby near the den and stepped away. After a few quick sniffs, the mother wolf accepted the boy and named him Mowgli.

For ten years, Mowgli lived with the wolves and was very happy. He loved his family, and he was a favorite among the other jungle animals.

But there was one jungle creature who did not like Mowgli. It was Shere Khan, a strong and cunning tiger. He had just returned to that part of the jungle. Shere Khan feared nothing but Man's gun and Man's fire. He had heard of the young Man-cub and believed that Mowgli would grow up to be a hunter. Shere Khan wanted to make sure that did not happen.

One night, the wolf elders met at Council Rock to discuss the tiger's return. "He will surely kill the boy," Akela, the wolf leader, told the council. Then he announced that Mowgli would have to leave the jungle.

When Bagheera heard the decision, he offered to help. "I know a Man-village where he'll be safe," he told the wolves.

"So be it," Akela said. "There is no time to lose."

158

Bagheera and Mowgli started out on their journey.

"We'll spend the night here," the panther said after a while. The pair settled down to sleep on a tree branch. They were both very tired and drifted off to sleep quickly.

Just then, Kaa the snake appeared. He thought Mowgli would make a tasty treat. Using his hypnotic eyes, Kaa put Mowgli in a trance. Then he wrapped the Man-cub in his coils.

Bagheera awoke and saw what was happening. He quickly jumped up and hit the snake on the head. *Smack!* With a bruised head and an empty belly, Kaa slithered away. Mowgli was safe—for now.

The next morning, Mowgli and Bagheera were awakened by loud rumbling and shaking. "A parade!" Mowgli shouted. He swung down from the tree to get a better look. It was a parade of elephants! Colonel Hathi, their leader, was in the front, giving orders and keeping everyone in line.

Mowgli wanted to march, too. He saw a baby elephant and ran over to join him. Now Mowgli was really having fun! But soon Colonel Hathi made them stop and line up for inspection. When he saw Mowgli, he asked, "What happened to your trunk?" Then he realized that Mowgli wasn't an elephant. "A Man-cub!" he cried.

160

Bagheera came to Mowgli's rescue. "The Man-cub is with me," he told the Colonel. "I'm taking him back to his village." When Hathi heard this, he calmed down and began to march again.

After the elephants left, Bagheera told Mowgli they had to keep moving. But the Man-cub was having fun and didn't want to leave the jungle. "Then from now on, you're on your own!" the panther told him.

Mowgli walked off and soon met a fun-loving bear named Baloo. They played together, sang together, and ate bananas and coconuts all day long.

Later, the two new friends floated down the river. Suddenly, a group of monkeys swooped down and picked Mowgli up. "Give me back my Man-cub!" shouted Baloo. But the monkeys ignored the bear and carried Mowgli to their leader, King Louie.

King Louie wanted to learn how to make fire, and he figured the Man-cub could teach him. Mowgli didn't know anything about making fire, though. He could not help Louie, and that made the king very angry.

In the meantime, Baloo found Bagheera. They searched for Mowgli and arrived just in time to save the Man-cub. Baloo disguised himself as an ape and started dancing with Louie. Soon, all the monkeys were dancing.

But when Baloo's costume fell off, the monkeys realized they'd been tricked. Baloo, Bagheera, and Mowgli quickly ran away to safety.

Later that night, Bagheera tried to convince Mowgli that the jungle was too dangerous for a young Man-cub. But Mowgli *still* didn't believe him, and he ran away again—right into Kaa!

The snake was just about to make Mowgli into a snack when Shere Khan interrupted. While Kaa and the tiger talked, Mowgli escaped and ran deep into the jungle.

Mowgli was finally all alone, but he was sad and tired. The Man-cub sat down on a rock to rest. Soon, four vultures flew down and started to tease him. But when they saw how lonely he was, they decided to be nicer. Just then, Shere Khan appeared. The vultures got scared and flew away quickly!

But Mowgli did not move. "You don't scare me, Shere Khan!" he said bravely.

Shere Khan lunged at the Man-cub, his razor-sharp claws flashing. But Baloo, who had been looking everywhere for Mowgli, arrived just in time! The bear grabbed Shere Khan by the tail and pulled him away from his friend. The vultures came back, picked up Mowgli, and flew him to a tree.

Suddenly, a bolt of lightning struck nearby and started a small fire. Mowgli climbed down from the tree, grabbed a burning branch, and snuck up behind Shere Khan. He tied the branch to Shere Khan's tail. The terrified tiger ran away, never to be seen again. Mowgli had saved the day!

Once again, Mowgli walked through the jungle with Baloo and Bagheera. All of a sudden, the Man-cub heard a new and beautiful sound. It was a girl from the Man-village, singing sweetly.

When Mowgli tried to impress the girl, she smiled at him and began to head toward the village. He followed her and turned to wave good-bye to Baloo and Bagheera.

The bear and panther watched Mowgli leave. Their Man-cub had found his true home at last . . . but they knew he would never forget his jungle friends.

Once upon a time, there was a pretty young girl named Cinderella. She lived with her widowed father. He loved her very much, but thought she needed a mother. So he married a woman with two daughters named Anastasia and Drizella. Not long after that, he died.

Cinderella's stepmother, Lady Tremaine, spent most of the family fortune. She forced Cinderella to become a servant and live in a cold, dark attic. Day in and day out, Cinderella did all of the household chores—from feeding the chickens to polishing the chandeliers. She waited on her stepsisters and stepmother hand and foot. Yet nothing she did ever pleased them.

No matter how mean her stepmother and stepsisters were, Cinderella was always cheerful. She made friends with the mice and birds and even sewed little outfits for them. Two of Cinderella's best friends were mice named Jaq and Gus.

One day, a messenger delivered an invitation to a royal ball. It was to be held that night at the palace. All the unmarried maidens in the kingdom were invited—the King wanted to find a wife for his son.

"Why, that means I can go, too!" Cinderella cried. Her stepsisters just laughed at her. They thought it was funny that a servant would think she could go to the ball.

"Well, why not?" asked Cinderella. "It says, 'By royal command, every eligible maiden is to attend.'"

Her stepmother looked at the invitation. "Well, I see no reason why you can't go," she said, "if you get all your work done and if you can find something suitable to wear."

Cinderella was delighted. She ran upstairs at once.

In her attic room, Cinderella opened her trunk and found a pink gown that had belonged to her mother. It was a little old-fashioned, but she knew she could make it into a beautiful dress.

All of a sudden, Cinderella's stepmother and stepsisters called for her. The gown would have to wait.

Lady Tremaine gave her stepdaughter a long list of chores to make certain that she wouldn't be able to go to the ball. Even if Cinderella finished, she wouldn't have time to fix the dress.

That evening, as Anastasia, Drizella, and Lady Tremaine were just about to leave for the ball, Cinderella went upstairs to her room. She had just finished her chores. Cinderella walked over to the window and looked out sadly at the palace in the distance.

But when she turned around, a surprise was waiting for her. The birds and mice had fixed her mother's old dress using ribbons and beads that Anastasia and Drizella had thrown away.

Cinderella was overjoyed. She thanked her friends and ran downstairs. When her stepsisters saw the gown and how beautiful Cinderella looked in it, they were furious.

"That's my sash!" Anastasia yelled as she ripped Cinderella's skirt.

"They're my beads!" Drizella cried as she pulled them from her stepsister's neck.

Cinderella's dress was in tatters. Knowing she couldn't go to the ball, she ran to the garden in tears.

Cinderella was sobbing on a garden bench when a kindly woman appeared. She comforted Cinderella and explained that she was her fairy godmother.

Then she waved her wand and said, "Bibbidi-Bobbidi-Boo." Suddenly, four mice were transformed into four white horses, and a big, round pumpkin became a glittering coach.

The Fairy Godmother waved her wand again and turned Cinderella's torn dress into a beautiful blue gown. Now she could go to the ball!

"Why, it's like a dream . . . a wonderful dream come true!" Cinderella exclaimed.

"You must understand, my dear," the Fairy Godmother said, "on the stroke of twelve, the spell will be broken. And everything will be as it was before."

And with that, the coach whisked Cinderella to the palace.

At the ball, the Prince met a lot of lovely maidens, but he didn't seem terribly interested in any of them. The King wondered if his son would meet anyone he wanted to marry.

Then Cinderella walked in. The Prince was enchanted by her beauty. He walked over to her, and they began to waltz. It was as if Cinderella was the only maiden in the room. The two danced all night. They even waltzed out to the moonlit balcony. Cinderella felt as if she were dreaming. I must be in love, she thought.

As the other guests watched the happy couple dance, they wondered who this beautiful young girl could be. No one had ever seen her before, but it was obvious she had stolen the Prince's heart.

As the clock struck
midnight, Cinderella
remembered what the
Fairy Godmother had
said. She quickly ran from
the palace before the spell was
broken. She was in such a hurry
that one of her glass slippers came
off as she rushed down the steps. The
Prince ran after her, but it was too late. Cinderella was gone,
and he hadn't even asked her name.

And Cinderella didn't know that the handsome man she had
been dancing with was actually the Prince!

The next day, Cinderella was busy doing her chores when
she overheard Lady Tremaine talking to her daughters. It
seemed the Grand Duke had been looking all night for the girl

who had lost her slipper at the ball. The Prince was madly in love with her.

"The Prince!" Cinderella exclaimed. She dropped the tray she was carrying. The man she'd been dancing with all night was the Prince? And he was madly in love with her? Could it be true?

"Not even the Prince knows who that girl is," Lady Tremaine said. "The glass slipper is their only clue. The Duke has been ordered to try it on every girl in the kingdom. And if one can be found whom the slipper fits, then by the King's command, that girl shall be the Prince's bride."

Cinderella was in shock. "His bride!" she whispered.

Her stepsisters began to fight over who would marry the Prince.

Cinderella started toward her room. She wanted to be wearing something prettier than work clothes when the Grand Duke arrived with the glass slipper. She walked down the hall, happier than she had ever been. Remembering her magical evening, she began to sing and waltz.

Lady Tremaine's eyes narrowed. She realized that Cinderella was the mysterious girl from the ball. She followed Cinderella upstairs and locked her in her attic room. She wanted one of her daughters to marry the Prince, not her stepdaughter!

When the Grand Duke arrived, Anastasia and Drizella both tried on the glass slipper, but their feet were much too big.

The Grand Duke was just about to leave when Cinderella rushed down the stairs. "Wait!" she called.

Gus and Jaq had stolen the key to Cinderella's room from her stepmother's pocket and freed their friend just in time.

Lady Tremaine was furious. She tripped the footman, and the glass slipper fell to the floor and shattered into many pieces.

Luckily, Cinderella had the matching slipper. She reached into her apron pocket and pulled it out. The slipper was a perfect fit!

The Grand Duke took Cinderella to the castle, where she married the Prince. And they lived happily ever after.

Once upon a time, two Dalmatians named Pongo and Perdita fell in love. Luckily, their owners, two humans named Roger and Anita, also fell in love. They all moved to a cozy house in London, and soon fifteen puppies were born.

Just after the puppies arrived, an old schoolmate of Anita's dropped by. Her name was Cruella De Vil. She wore a large fur coat, and her hair was half black and half white. She had heard about the puppies and wanted to buy them.

Roger and Anita weren't interested, but Cruella insisted. She even got out her checkbook. As Roger and Cruella argued, the woman shook her pen and splashed ink all over him.

"We're not selling the puppies . . . and that's final!" he yelled.

Cruella stormed out, furious.

Pongo and Perdita were delighted with the puppies. One was so tiny, they didn't think he would make it. But somehow he survived. When his spots came in, they formed the shape of a horseshoe on his back, so he was named Lucky. Another puppy had a black patch over his eye, so he was called Patch. One of their brothers was named Rolly, and they had a sister named Penny.

The puppies all liked to play together. Some nights, they even watched TV. They were a happy family.

One day, Roger and Anita took Pongo and Perdita for a walk. While they were out, Horace and Jasper, two of Cruella's henchmen, went to their house, pretending to be from the electric company. When the two men got inside, they locked Nanny, the housekeeper, in a room, put the puppies in a large bag, and left. Then they drove out to Cruella's country estate and waited to hear from her.

When Nanny finally escaped, she saw that the puppy basket was empty and immediately called the police.

Soon Pongo and Perdita returned. They could not believe their eyes—their puppies had been stolen!

Pongo and Perdita knew that the Twilight Bark was their only hope. They got Roger and Anita to take them to a park, where they could bark the message to all the dogs in London. Those dogs would pass it along to the animals who lived in the country. Maybe one of them would have seen the puppies.

"Fifteen Dalmatian puppies stolen!" Pongo barked. A Great Dane heard his plea and spread the news. Before long, dogs all over England had heard about the stolen puppies.

Later that night, the Twilight Bark reached a quiet farm, where a cat named Sergeant Tibs heard it. He awakened the Colonel, an old English sheepdog, and told him about the dognapping.

Sergeant Tibs thought that he'd heard barking at the old De Vil place. He and the Colonel set out for the gloomy mansion.

The sheepdog and cat arrived at Cruella's place, and Sergeant Tibs went inside. He discovered the missing Dalmatians, plus eighty-four others! There were ninety-nine puppies altogether!

He told the Colonel to use the Twilight Bark to pass along the news that the pups had been located. When Pongo and Perdita heard, they set out for the countryside right away.

Meanwhile, Tibs and the Colonel kept a close watch over the puppies. Cruella soon arrived, and they found out that she wanted to use the puppies for fur coats!

"I don't care how you kill the little beasts, but do it. And do it now!" she told Jasper and Horace. After she left, the two men decided to finish watching TV before they did anything.

Luckily, Tibs had heard the whole thing. He came up with a plan to help the pups escape through a hole in the wall. The cat led the Dalmatians down the stairs and hid them under the staircase. They were trembling with fright.

Jasper and Horace realized the pups were gone and started to search for them. Just as they found the puppies, Pongo and Perdita arrived and attacked the two bad men.

The puppies ran outside to safety. Perdita and Pongo soon followed, having momentarily foiled Horace and Jasper.

Their fifteen puppies called out to them. "Mother! Dad! I sure missed you. Here we are!"

"Oh, my darlings. My darlings!" Perdita gushed, thankful to be reunited with her children.

When Pongo and Perdita learned about Cruella's plans for the other Dalmatians, they decided to take all ninety-nine puppies back to London. They would have to be careful, though, for they knew Cruella and her men would be searching for them.

The Dalmatians thanked the Colonel and Tibs for their help and started off through the snow. When the dogs realized Jasper and Horace were following them, they walked on the frozen river so as not to leave any tracks. Soon, they heard a truck coming and hid under a bridge.

The truck stopped, and Horace got out. "What if they went down the froze-up creek so's not to leave their tracks?" he asked Jasper.

"Dogs ain't that smart," Jasper replied. Horace got back in the truck and the two drove off.

The dogs started walking down the frozen creek again. But it was a long journey. Before long, the puppies were exhausted and hungry. After a while, Lucky couldn't walk anymore, so his father carried him.

Luckily, a collie soon met them and led them to a dairy farm. The puppies rested in the hay for a while and drank some milk.

The food made the puppies strong enough to continue to a town called Dinsford, where a Labrador brought them to a blacksmith's shop to rest. Later, they would board a truck that was bound for London.

While they were waiting, Cruella arrived. Pongo knew that the puppies couldn't walk right by her to get on the truck. But they were too small to travel the rest of the way on foot.

Lucky and Patch got in a fight while their father tried to come up with a plan. As they tussled, the puppies rolled around in the ashes of the fireplace. Soon they were black with soot. Pongo glanced over at them and came up with an idea—all the puppies should cover themselves in ashes. That way, Cruella wouldn't recognize them.

"Come on kids, roll in the soot!" he cried, and the puppies romped around until their fur was completely covered.

Since the pups were disguised, Pongo and Perdita thought it was safe to board the truck. They walked right by Cruella. But just as the last group of puppies were about to hop on, a clump of snow fell and washed the soot off one of them.

From her car, Cruella could see it was a Dalmatian.

"Jasper! Horace!" she yelled to her men, who had arrived in Dinsford in their own car. "There they go! After them!"

The truck with the puppies took off and Cruella zoomed after it. She tried to run it off the road, even driving through a barricade. But while Cruella was chasing the truck, Jasper and Horace were coming at it from a different direction. They didn't see her car. The truck avoided both cars, but Cruella, Jasper, and Horace crashed into each other.

Cruella's fancy car was ruined. There was no way she'd be able to get the puppies now.

Pongo and Perdita and all ninety-nine puppies arrived back in London safely and hurried home.

Roger and Anita were surprised to see so many puppies. They cleaned the soot off them and began to count. With Pongo and Perdita, there were 101 Dalmatians!

"What'll we do with them?" Anita asked.

"We'll keep them," Roger answered. "We'll buy a big place in the country, and we'll have a plantation," he said. "A Dalmatian plantation!"

And that's exactly what they did.

One December evening in 1910, a businessman named Jim hurried home through the snow. He was very excited about the Christmas present he'd just picked out for his wife.

When Jim arrived, he presented the gift. "It's for you, Darling."

"Oh, Jim, dear," said his wife. Before she could open the box, the lid came off all by itself, revealing an adorable cocker spaniel.

The puppy looked up at the happy couple. "You like her, darling?" Jim asked.

"What a perfectly beautiful little lady," his wife replied.

So the puppy came to know her new family as Jim Dear and Darling. And they decided to name her Lady.

By summer, Lady enjoyed going for afternoon walks with Darling. But one day, no matter how much Lady begged, her owner would not go outside. Lady soon learned that Darling was expecting a baby.

In the yard, Lady told her good friends Jock, a Scottish terrier, and Trusty, a bloodhound, the news.

At that moment, a scruffy dog named Tramp wandered down the street. Tramp had no home and did not know what it was like to belong to a loving family. He'd overheard what Lady had said to others. "When a baby moves in, the dog moves out," he told her.

Jock growled. Tramp moved on, but Lady thought about what he'd said.

Soon the baby arrived, and Lady had one more wonderful person to care for and love. She decided that Tramp had been wrong.

Several weeks later, Lady noticed that Jim Dear and Darling had packed their bags. "Don't worry, old girl," Jim told Lady. "We'll be back in a few days."

"And Aunt Sarah will be here," Darling added.

"With you here to help her—" Jim began.

Just then, the doorbell rang. It was Aunt Sarah, and she'd brought her cats, Si and Am. After Jim Dear and Darling left, the cats began to act up. They attacked the canary and the goldfish, and ruined Darling's pretty living room. Lady tried to stop them, but Si and Am made it look like she had attacked them and made the mess.

Aunt Sarah was very angry with Lady. She took her to the pet store and told the clerk, "I want a muzzle. A good, strong muzzle."

Aunt Sarah held Lady down, while the clerk fastened a muzzle around her head. But it was more than Lady could bear. After all, she hadn't done anything wrong. So she yanked her leash from Aunt Sarah's hands and ran away as fast as she could.

When Lady stopped to catch her breath, she realized she was in a strange part of town. A pack of mean dogs surrounded her.

Just then, Tramp appeared. He saw that Lady was in danger. He bravely fought the stray dogs, finally chasing them away.

"Ya poor kid!" said Tramp. He took Lady to the zoo, where a friendly beaver chewed through the muzzle strap.

That night, Tramp took Lady to one of his favorite spots—Tony's Restaurant. "The very place for a very special occasion," said Tramp.

Tony, the owner, served the meal. "The best spaghetti in town," he said. By candlelight, the two dogs shared the delicious pasta. Tony sang to them while they ate. Lady and Tramp did not even notice that they were eating the same long piece of spaghetti until they reached the middle and their lips met in a kiss!

Later, Lady and Tramp fell asleep in the park. The next morning, they woke up when a rooster crowed. "I should have been home hours ago," Lady said.

Tramp did not believe in having to do anything or having to be anywhere. He did not understand why Lady would want to leave.

"Open your eyes to what a dog's life can really be!" Tramp told Lady. "Ever chase chickens?"

he asked as he rushed into a yard filled with the squawking birds.

"We shouldn't!" Lady cried. She started to follow Tramp, but a net suddenly surrounded her. A dogcatcher put her in a truck and drove her to the pound.

The dogs at the pound began to tease Lady. She was afraid and very upset.

Peg, a fluffy Pekingese, came to her rescue. "Can't you see the poor kid's scared enough?" she asked.

Lady was relieved when Aunt Sarah arrived.

Aunt Sarah brought Lady home and chained her to the doghouse in the backyard.

Soon, Tramp came to apologize. "I thought you were right behind me. Honest!" he said. But Lady was too upset to listen. She was embarrassed that she had been locked up, and she blamed him.

As Tramp left, Lady saw a rat scurry up a vine to the baby's room. Lady chased after it, but she was stopped by her chain. She barked as loudly as she could. Aunt Sarah stuck her head out the window. "Stop that racket!" she yelled.

Tramp came running. "What's wrong?" he asked.

"A rat!" Lady cried. "Upstairs in the baby's room!"

Tramp ran inside the house. Lady pulled at her chain until it broke, then rushed upstairs to help fight the rat.

Tramp accidentally knocked over the crib as he raced after the rodent. Luckily, the baby was fine. Lady rushed in and watched over the baby while Tramp fought the rat behind the curtains. Finally, Tramp emerged and limped toward Lady, licking his paw.

Aunt Sarah came to the nursery and saw Lady and Tramp standing by the baby. "You vicious brutes!" she cried. Then she called the pound to take Tramp away. She hadn't noticed the dead rat by the curtains.

The dogcatcher arrived and loaded Tramp into his wagon. Just then, Jim Dear and Darling came home. "What's going on here?" Jim wondered.

Lady led Jim Dear to the nursery, and he lifted the drapes.

"A rat!" Aunt Sarah shrieked.

Outside the house, Trusty and Jock overheard Aunt Sarah scream. They realized that Tramp had been misjudged. "We've got to stop that wagon!" Trusty exclaimed.

They soon caught up with the dogcatcher. Trusty barked very loudly. The horses got spooked and reared. The wagon tipped over—right onto poor Trusty!

Then, Jim Dear and Lady arrived in a taxi. Lady found Tramp in the back of the overturned wagon, and they happily touched noses. Then Lady saw Trusty lying in the snow. She hurried over. He had a broken leg, but he would be all right.

By the time Christmas arrived, Trusty was doing just fine. His leg was bandaged, but he was able to walk over with Jock to visit Lady and her new family.

Jim Dear and Darling had been so grateful to Tramp for saving the baby that they asked him to live with them. Lady and Tramp had four adorable puppies, and they had never been happier.

They knew how lucky they were to have such a nice home—and such a wonderful family to share it with.

Disney's

The Prince
and the
Pauper

Once upon a time, there was a kindly king who ruled with fairness and generosity. His son, the Prince, was busy with his studies, but he loved the kingdom, too. It was a time of great peace, and the people of the land were very happy.

But then the King grew sick and could no longer watch over his people.

The greedy leader of the King's guards, Captain Pete, saw the King's illness as his chance to get rich. Day after day, the captain and his soldiers took money and other valuable objects from the people of the kingdom. Neither the King nor the Prince knew what Captain Pete was doing, and the King's subjects kept getting poorer and poorer.

One very cold morning, two peasants named Mickey and Goofy watched as Captain Pete drove the royal coach past them. When Mickey's dog, Pluto, spotted some sausages hanging from the coach, he ran after it. The dog was very hungry because Captain Pete and his men had taken so much of the kingdom's food. The coach disappeared through the palace gates, with Pluto following close behind.

"Stop!" Mickey shouted as he ran after his dog. "Come back!" But it was too late. The gates had shut behind Pluto.

When Mickey got to the gate, he asked if he could go inside to get his dog. The guard was about to say no when he got a good look at the peasant's face. "Your Majesty," the guard said, gasping. He quickly waved Mickey inside.

Mickey didn't care what the guard had called him. He just wanted his dog back.

Meanwhile, inside the palace, the Prince was sitting through another boring history lesson with Professor Horace. To amuse himself, he took out a peashooter and aimed it at his valet, Donald. *Whack!* The Prince landed a shot right on Donald's head. *Whack!* Another one hit the valet's bottom.

Professor Horace was just about to scold the Prince when he heard a commotion outside. The Prince ran to the window and saw Captain Pete holding up a bag with a peasant trapped inside. It was Mickey! The captain had found him wandering around and captured him. The Prince ordered Pete to let the captive out of the bag and send him inside.

Pete sent Mickey into the castle, but the young pauper got lost in one of the many halls. Mickey was so busy looking around, he stumbled right into a suit of armor. The suit's helmet fell off and dropped down onto his head. *Clang!*

Just then, the Prince entered the hall, and another helmet fell down—onto *his* head! Neither the Prince nor the pauper could see where they were going. They walked blindly until— *bang!*—they crashed into each other. Slowly, they lifted the fronts of their helmets. "You look just like me!" they shouted in unison.

The Prince couldn't believe his luck. This was just the chance he had been waiting for! Now he could leave the boring palace and no one would know. He quickly convinced Mickey to trade places with him. To Mickey, the idea of living in a luxurious palace as a prince sounded amazing. What harm could it do? They swapped clothes, and the Prince headed for the door.

"I'll be back in the blink of an eye," he promised. Then he left, eager to explore the world.

The Prince made it outside and past the royal guard, but then he ran into Pluto. The dog sniffed him a few times and walked off. He hadn't been fooled. The Prince was *not* his master.

When Goofy saw the Prince, he thought he was Mickey and began to talk to him. The Prince ran off, leaving a confused Goofy behind.

Back at the palace, instead of eating tasty food and being treated royally, Mickey was trying to follow the Prince's geography lesson. It was not going well.

The Prince wasn't doing any better outside the castle walls. He tried playing fetch with some dogs, but they chased him over a fence. Disappointed, he went to the marketplace. There he saw one of the captain's guards stealing food from poor people. "Halt! I am the Prince," he cried, holding up his royal ring. Then he climbed atop the cart and gave the food to the hungry peasants.

The peasants were overjoyed. They hadn't eaten in a long while.

When the guard saw the Prince's ring, he rushed back to tell Pete what had happened. When Captain Pete heard the news, he came up with a plan. He would get rid of the real prince and make the fake one do whatever he demanded. That way Pete would rule the kingdom!

Meanwhile, Goofy had found the Prince walking about town and brought him to his house. A while later, the church bells tolled throughout the land. The King had died. The Prince told Goofy that he was not his friend, Mickey, but the new ruler. He showed Goofy his ring. "I must go to the palace right away," he said. "I will miss my father greatly, but now it is my duty to take over as king." Then he leaped out of his chair and headed toward the door.

But Captain Pete was waiting for him just outside.

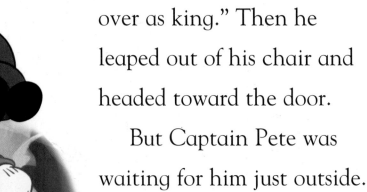

The guards quickly captured the Prince, brought him to the palace, and threw him into the dungeon. Donald was already inside.

"I see your royal ring," Pete said from outside the Prince's cell. "But it won't do you any good. As soon as the pauper is crowned king, I shall unmask him as an impostor and rule the kingdom myself!" With an evil laugh, he left.

The situation looked hopeless for the Prince . . . and the entire kingdom.

Just then, a strange-looking guard came to the dungeon door. It was Goofy! "Sit tight, little buddy," he said as he got the Prince out of his cell. But Pete's guards were close behind. Luckily, the Prince, Goofy, and Donald escaped after a long chase.

Meanwhile, Mickey was trying to avoid being crowned king. He knew that Captain Pete would keep stealing from the people of the kingdom, so he stopped the ceremony. "I'm the Prince. So whatever I order must be done, right?" Mickey asked the

man who was about to crown him. The man nodded, and Mickey ordered the guards to seize Pete.

But Pete was ready for this. "He is not the Prince!" yelled the wicked captain. "He's an impostor! Seize him!"

"*I'm* not an impostor, though!" came a voice from a high balcony. It was the real prince!

Everyone gasped and looked up in time to see the Prince
swing down to the ground on a chandelier. Swords slashed and
fists flew as Mickey, the Prince, and their friends struggled
against Pete and the guards. Pluto even took a bite out of Pete's
pants! Soon the fight was over. The evil captain was arrested,
and the Prince was crowned king.

The kingdom was once again in kind, caring hands. With Mickey and Goofy by his side, the new king ruled . . . happily ever after.

The crew of the *Susan Constant* took one last look at London before setting sail for the new land in search of gold. They were led by John Ratcliffe, a mean-spirited and ambitious governor. But the rest of the crew was a friendly bunch. Lon, Ben, Thomas, and the others hoped to make their fortunes, and the brave John Smith had been hired to fight the Indians.

The months at sea were long and hard. During one storm, a huge wave swept Thomas overboard. In a flash, John Smith tied a rope around his own waist and dived after him. The rest of the crew hauled them both to safety.

Ratcliffe heard the commotion and went on deck. He reminded the sailors that freedom and riches awaited them. "Not even a band of bloodthirsty Indians shall stand in our way!" he exclaimed. Then he returned to his comfortable cabin.

"No need to worry about Indians," added Smith. "I'll take care of them."

In the new land, warriors from the Algonquin Indian tribe were returning home from battle. They were celebrating a recent victory over another tribe, and a group from the village had gathered to greet them. The noble chief, Powhatan, told his people of the admirable courage of the young brave named Kocoum.

At the celebration, Powhatan looked for his beloved daughter, Pocahontas. He sighed. Pocahontas was adventurous like her mother had been, following the wind wherever it took her. Powhatan wasn't surprised that she wasn't there to greet him. She was always off on her own, exploring. He wondered where she could be.

Pocahontas was in the woods, admiring the view from the edge of a waterfall with her pals Meeko, a raccoon, and Flit, a hummingbird. Her best friend, Nakoma, appeared in a canoe at the bottom of the waterfall. "Pocahontas, your father's back!" she called. "Come down here!"

With that, Pocahontas dived over the waterfall and swam to the canoe. "That's not exactly what I meant," Nakoma said. "What were you doing up there, anyway?"

"I was thinking about my dream," Pocahontas replied. "I know it means something." Then she and Nakoma rowed toward the village.

Later, Pocahontas greeted Powhatan. "Father, for many nights now, I've had a strange dream. I think it is telling me something's about to happen."

"It is," her father said with a smile. "The courageous Kocoum has asked for your hand in marriage." Then he gave Pocahontas a necklace that her mother had worn on their wedding day.

Pocahontas did not think her dream had been about marriage. Besides, Kocoum was so serious all the time—he didn't seem right for her. Pocahontas wanted to make her father happy, yet she knew she had to follow her heart.

She visited Grandmother Willow, the ancient tree spirit by the river. "I've been having this dream," Pocahontas explained. "And I'm not sure what it means."

"Tell me all about it, child," said the tree.

"I'm running through the woods and in front of me is a spinning arrow," said Pocahontas. "Oh, Grandmother Willow, should I marry Kocoum, or is my dream telling me something else? Which path should I take?"

"Your mother asked the same question," said the kindly tree. "And I told her, 'If you listen to the spirits, they will guide you.'"

As Pocahontas thought about what Grandmother Willow had said, she looked seaward and noticed some strange white clouds. But they weren't clouds at all—they were the sails of the *Susan Constant.*

Aboard the ship, the tired crew was glad to see land again. John Smith soon went ashore to explore. Pocahontas hid on the cliff to watch him.

When Smith climbed too close to Pocahontas's hiding place, Meeko ran up to him. Smith gave the raccoon a biscuit and started to walk toward Pocahontas.

Just then, a bugle sounded. John Smith went to find the other settlers. When he did, Govenor Ratcliffe was planting a British flag in the soil to claim the land. Then the governor ordered the others to unload the ship, build a fort, and dig for gold.

But John Smith was eager to explore the land, so he set off again. Pocahontas followed him quietly. Before long, the two came face-to-face. When Pocahontas ran away, Smith followed her. Then he spoke to her, and Pocahontas remembered Grandmother Willow's advice. He sounded kind, though she couldn't understand him.

After spending some time together, they figured out how to communicate. Pocahontas even taught Smith some Indian words, including "hello" and "good-bye."

As Pocahontas showed Smith her world, he realized that they had a lot to learn from each other. Just as their hands accidentally touched, the sound of beating drums interrupted them.

When Pocahontas returned to her village, she discovered that the Indians knew about the settlers and planned to fight them. Meanwhile, John Smith met with the other settlers to convince them to keep the peace. But Ratcliffe hadn't discovered any gold yet, and was sure the Indians had hidden it somewhere. Both sides were determined to fight.

That night, Smith and Pocahontas met up near Grandmother Willow and shared a tender kiss.

At that moment, Kocoum charged from a hiding place, swinging his tomahawk at Smith. "Leave him alone!" shouted Pocahontas. The two men began to fight. Then Thomas suddenly appeared. While trying to protect Smith, he shot Kocoum. Smith ordered Thomas to run away. Seconds later, a band of Indians captured Smith and brought him back to their village.

Powhatan decided that John Smith would die at sunrise. The chief was very angry with Pocahontas. "Because of your foolishness Kocoum is dead!" he cried.

Later, Pocahontas secretly went to see John Smith. "It would have been better if we'd never met," she told him.

"I'd rather die tomorrow than live a hundred years without having known you," he replied.

"I can't leave you," Pocahontas said tearfully.

"You never will," Smith said. "No matter what happens to me, I'll always be with you."

Pocahontas visited the ancient tree again. "I followed the wrong path, Grandmother Willow." Then Meeko gave her a compass. He had taken it from Smith's bag, thinking it was food. "Spinning arrow," Pocahontas said thoughtfully.

"It's the arrow from your dream," Grandmother Willow said.

Upon hearing that, Pocahontas turned and ran swiftly back to the village. She had to stop her father from killing John Smith. She had to make things right.

Ratcliffe and the angry settlers arrived at the village just as Chief Powhatan was about to kill Smith.

Pocahontas appeared at the same time. "No! I love him, Father!" she shouted. "Look around you. This is where the path of hatred has brought us."

The chief looked at the angry men on both sides. "If there is to be more killing, it will not start with me," he said as he released John Smith.

Ratcliffe shot at Powhatan anyway. Smith jumped in front of the chief, taking the bullet himself. The other settlers captured Ratcliffe and led him toward the ship.

John Smith was told he had to return to London to treat his wounds. "Come with me?" he asked Pocahontas.

"I'm needed here," she replied bravely.

"But I can't leave you," he said.

"You never will," replied Pocahontas.

As the ship sailed out to sea, Smith made the Indian sign that Pocahontas had taught him for good-bye. Standing on the cliff where she had first seen his ship, Pocahontas repeated the gesture.

"A-nah," whispered John Smith.

"Good-bye," Pocahontas said softly.

*L*ong ago, a beautiful girl was born to a king and queen. They named her Aurora.

To celebrate his daughter's long-awaited birth, King Stefan declared a holiday for the entire kingdom. People came from near and far to bring gifts to the child. The neighboring King Hubert and his young son, Phillip, came to see the princess. The two kings were great friends and wished to join their kingdoms in peace and prosperity. They decided that Princess Aurora and Prince Phillip would marry when they grew up.

At the king's invitation, three good fairies named Flora, Fauna, and Merryweather came to the celebration. Each had a magical gift for the princess.

Flora, the fairy dressed in red, waved her wand over the baby's cradle. "My gift shall be the gift of beauty," she said.

"My gift shall be the gift of song," said Fauna, the fairy in green.

But before Merryweather could speak, an evil fairy named Maleficent appeared. She was angry because the king had not invited her to the celebration.

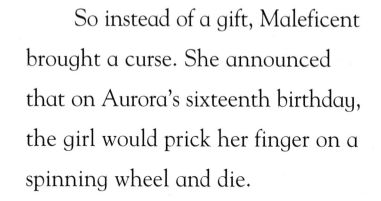

So instead of a gift, Maleficent brought a curse. She announced that on Aurora's sixteenth birthday, the girl would prick her finger on a spinning wheel and die.

The king's guards tried to capture Maleficent, but she vanished in a cloud of smoke and fire.

Fortunately, Merryweather, the fairy in blue, had not yet offered her gift. She could not reverse the evil curse, but she cast a spell that would make Aurora fall asleep when she pricked her finger. That way the princess wouldn't die. "And from this slumber you shall wake when True Love's Kiss the spell shall break," Merryweather announced.

To keep Aurora safe, the three good fairies said they would disguise themselves as peasants, raise the princess in a cottage, and rename her Briar Rose. The fairies told her parents they'd bring Aurora home on her sixteenth birthday. King Stefan and the queen sadly agreed.

When Maleficent discovered Aurora was missing, she ordered her evil soldiers to search the entire kingdom.

As the years passed, Briar Rose never once suspected she was a princess. She thought the fairies were her aunts, and they all lived happily in their cottage.

On the morning of Briar Rose's sixteenth birthday, the fairies decided to throw her a surprise party. They were discussing the cake and gift when Briar Rose walked in.

"What are you three dears up to?" the girl teased.

"Uh . . . uh . . . we want you to go pick some berries," Merryweather blurted out.

"Lots of berries," Fauna added.

"But I picked berries yesterday," Briar Rose said sweetly.

The fairies smiled and sent the girl on her way so they could start to get everything ready.

The fairies had stopped using magic long ago for fear that Maleficent might discover Aurora's hiding place. But because the curse was about to end—and they weren't very good at baking and sewing—Merryweather suggested they use their magic wands. But Flora and Fauna refused.

"I'm going to bake the cake," Fauna said. "I'm going to make it fifteen layers, with pink and blue forget-me-nots."

"And I'm making the dress," Flora declared.

Fauna's cake turned out so lopsided that she had to prop it up with a broom, but then the icing and candles ran down the broom handle.

And when Merryweather tried on the dress that Flora had sewn, it practically fell apart! "Perhaps if I added a few more ruffles?" Flora asked.

Finally, the fairies pulled out their magic wands and made everything perfect.

The dress and cake were fit for a princess, but sparks from the fairies' wands had come out of the chimney just as Maleficent's pet raven was flying by. The bird saw the flashes of magic and realized that the princess had been hiding at the cottage.

Meanwhile, Briar Rose wandered through the woods and began to sing. A handsome young man, who had been riding through the woods, heard her lovely voice and joined her. Briar Rose did not realize that he was Prince Phillip, but as they walked and sang together, she knew she loved him with all her heart.

Hours later, Briar Rose returned to the cottage. She was delighted by her birthday presents, but even more excited about the handsome man she'd met that day. "Just wait till you meet him," she told the fairies.

Sadly, the fairies told her who she really was and that she was already betrothed to Prince Phillip. Because of that, she could never see her handsome stranger again.

"Tonight we're taking you back to your father, King Stefan," Flora told the stunned princess.

Once the fairies thought it was safe, they returned Aurora to the castle. Left alone to prepare to see her parents, the princess wept. But Maleficent was waiting for her. Immediately, she placed Aurora in a trance and lured her to a lonely tower. The princess pricked her finger on a spinning wheel and fell into a deep sleep.

To save Aurora's parents from terrible heartache, the good fairies put everyone in the castle to sleep.

Meanwhile, Maleficent had figured out Prince Phillip was

the only one who could break the spell and wake the princess with True Love's Kiss. So she found him and locked him in her dungeon.

The three fairies soon realized that Maleficent had trapped the prince. They flew to the evil fairy's dungeon and helped Prince Phillip escape. "Arm thyself with this enchanted Shield of Virtue and this mighty Sword of Truth," Flora told him.

When Prince Phillip approached Aurora's castle, he saw that Maleficent had covered the walls with thick, thorny branches. He used the magical sword to cut through them.

Maleficent realized that the prince might defeat her and turned herself into a fire-breathing dragon. "Now you shall deal with me, oh prince!" she screeched.

The prince charged toward the large dragon, his sword raised. Maleficent breathed a huge blast of flame toward him. Phillip blocked it with his magical shield, but the branches around him caught fire. Then the dragon chased him to the edge of a cliff. He was trapped.

The dragon was about to breathe more fire, when all of a sudden the three fairies came to Phillip's rescue. "Now Sword of Truth fly swift and sure . . ." the fairies said, as they sprinkled fairy dust onto the sword.

Phillip threw the sword at the dragon, and the beast plunged over the cliff.

The prince had defeated the dragon, and Maleficent was no more.

Prince Phillip raced to the tower and found Aurora sleeping peacefully. He kissed her tenderly. The princess opened her eyes and smiled at her true love.

Everyone in the castle woke up, too. The king and queen were overjoyed to see their daughter again. Aurora was happier than she'd ever been. She had reunited with her family, and she and her true love would be together forever.

Disney's

THE
HUNCHBACK
OF NOTRE DAME

Long ago in the city of Paris, a young man lived in the bell tower of the great Cathedral of Notre Dame. His name was Quasimodo, and it was his job to ring the cathedral bell. His back was hunched in an odd shape, but he was strong and kind. Because he stayed hidden in the tower, Quasimodo's only friends were the stone gargoyles that had been carved into the church. They came to life, but only in front of him.

Quasimodo's master, Judge Claude Frollo, was a mean man. Years earlier, he had accidentally killed a gypsy—Quasimodo's mother—and did not want anyone to discover what had happened. So he kept the hunchback hidden and told him he was a monster.

Many years passed. Quasimodo grew up in the tower, always watching the people below, wishing he could leave and meet some of them. Then one day, everything changed.

Once a year, all of Paris prepared for the day known as the
Festival of Fools. On that day, people paraded around the city
dressed in scary masks and funny costumes. The person with
the best mask was crowned the King of Fools.

Up in the cathedral, the gargoyles watched the merriment
in the streets below. One of them asked Quasimodo if he
had ever thought of leaving the tower. "Sure," the
hunchback replied, "but I'd never fit in."

The gargoyles insisted that the festival
was the perfect time for him to explore the
city. Quasimodo finally agreed and put on
a hooded robe to wear as a disguise.
Eager to see the world, the hunchback
grabbed a rope and swung down into
the crowds below. He had never had
so much freedom—or been so happy.

On the streets, everyone was so busy having fun, no one noticed Quasimodo wandering around. He watched the parade and saw many things for the first time. He could not believe how bright and colorful everything looked up close. It was his first trip outside the cathedral, and he was having a perfect day!

Then he met Esmeralda, a dancing gypsy. Frollo had told him that gypsies were bad, but Quasimodo thought Esmeralda was the most beautiful thing he had ever seen. He just hoped that she did not think he was a monster.

Quasimodo was not the only one who had seen her though. That very day, the new Captain of the Guard arrived in Paris. His name was Phoebus, and he was strong and handsome. He also noticed Esmeralda's beauty.

Later that day, Quasimodo was crowned King of Fools for having the best mask. The crowd laughed—until they saw the mask was not a mask at all—it was his real face. Then they became very mean and tied him up. They called him names and threw things at him. Quasimodo cried for help, but no one stepped forward. Esmeralda was outraged. She ran to the hunchback and freed him.

Frollo saw what Esmeralda had done and was very angry. He ordered Phoebus to arrest her. But Esmeralda and her gray goat, Djali, ran into the cathedral, where they would be safe.

"Set one foot outside, and you're my prisoner," Frollo warned her. Then he posted a guard at each door. Esmeralda stayed inside and went to find Quasimodo, who had returned to the cathedral, ashamed and embarrassed.

Quasimodo thought Esmeralda was very nice. She had freed him when no one else would, and she was easy to talk to. He decided his master must be wrong about gypsies. And if Frollo was wrong about Esmeralda, maybe he had been wrong about Quasimodo, too. Maybe he wasn't a monster after all! The hunchback decided to help the beautiful gypsy escape.

Quasimodo carried Esmeralda and Djali down the side of the cathedral. When they reached the street, Esmeralda asked her new friend to come with her to a gypsy hideaway called the Court of Miracles. Quasimodo would not leave, so she gave him a special amulet that would help him find her if he ever needed to. "This will show you the way," she promised. "When you wear this woven band, you hold the city in your hand." Then, she hurried away.

272

When Frollo learned that Esmeralda had escaped, he ordered Phoebus to burn down the home of anyone who had helped the gypsies or who might be keeping Esmeralda's location a secret.

Phoebus refused, so Frollo's soldiers started to set buildings on fire. The captain could not stand to see anyone hurt, so he rescued a family that was trapped in a burning building. Frollo was furious and tried to kill him. As Phoebus tried to get away, one of Frollo's archers hit him in the back with an arrow.

Esmeralda found the wounded captain and brought him to the bell tower. She asked Quasimodo to hide him. The hunchback agreed, for he could see that the two were in love. Even though Quasimodo knew Esmeralda would never care for him the same way, he would still do anything for her.

THE HUNCHBACK OF NOTRE DAME

Once Esmeralda left, Frollo went to the bell tower to try and trick Quasimodo into telling him how to find her. "I know where her hideout is," he lied. "And tomorrow at dawn, I attack with a thousand men." With that, Frollo left.

Quasimodo and Phoebus knew they had to warn Esmeralda, but the hunchback was scared to stand up to his master.

"You must do what you think is right," Phoebus said.

Quasimodo thought about it. Esmeralda had been very kind to him, and this was his chance to repay her. He ran after the captain. "I'm not doing it for you," the hunchback said. "I'm doing it for her."

Quasimodo knew he could find Esmeralda at the Court of Miracles. Using the map on the amulet, he and Phoebus set out to find her. They did not realize that Frollo and his soldiers were following them.

Soon after Quasimodo and Phoebus had arrived at the gypsy hideout, Frollo burst in and arrested them all. Esmeralda and Phoebus were led off to prison, while Quasimodo was chained up in the cathedral's tower.

But chains could not hold the determined bell ringer. Breaking free, he rushed to the prison, arriving just as Frollo was about to kill Esmeralda. Quasimodo rescued her and raced back to the safety of the bell tower. Lifting her up in his arms, Quasimodo shouted down to Frollo and his men to leave them alone.

Frollo could not believe the hunchback had betrayed him again! He ordered his men to seize the cathedral. But Quasimodo had friends. With the help of Phoebus, who had escaped from prison, and the gargoyles, the hunchback set fire to a huge vat of lead he found in the tower. Then they poured it down on Frollo and his soldiers. Quasimodo had saved the day!

With Frollo defeated, the friends walked out of the cathedral and into the sunlight. A crowd was waiting, and they cheered when the hunchback appeared. The bell ringer who had thought he was a monster was now a great hero!

One spring day, a cardboard box filled with kittens was left on the sidewalk in New York City. The kittens were very cute, and all were adopted quickly, except for a fluffy little orange one. Alone, scared, and *very* hungry, the kitten stuck his head

over the edge of the box and looked around. Then he jumped out and set off to find food. Before long, some mean dogs began to chase him. He luckily escaped.

Later, he smelled something delicious—hot dogs! Dodger, a street-smart dog who was standing nearby, had smelled the hot dogs, too. He came up with a plan and asked the kitten to help. In return, they would share the food. But when the kitten distracted the vendor, Dodger grabbed the meat and took off . . . alone!

"Wait!" cried the kitten. "Half those dogs are mine!" But Dodger just laughed and kept running. He raced through alleys and over fences and finally ended up down at the docks, where he slipped into a room on a rundown barge.

But there was something Dodger did not know: the kitten had followed him! Hiding up on the deck, the kitten peeked through a hole. Inside, he saw Dodger talking to a group of dogs— Tito the Chihuahua, Francis the bulldog, Einstein the Great Dane, and a lovely hound named Rita. Dodger was busy bragging about how he had gotten the hot dogs all by himself.

Suddenly, there was a loud crash. Dodger and the other dogs looked up in surprise as the little kitten fell through the ceiling!

The kitten was surrounded. He was scared, and his heart was pounding. He had never been that close to so many dogs before. "I just followed this dog. . . ." he said in a shaky voice.

"Relax, kid," Rita told him gently. The kitten took a deep breath. He was about to ask for his half of the hot dogs when a man walked into the room holding a box of dog biscuits. The dogs rushed over to greet him. The man's name was Fagin. He lived on the barge and took care of the dogs. Usually he was happy-go-lucky, but now he looked sad.

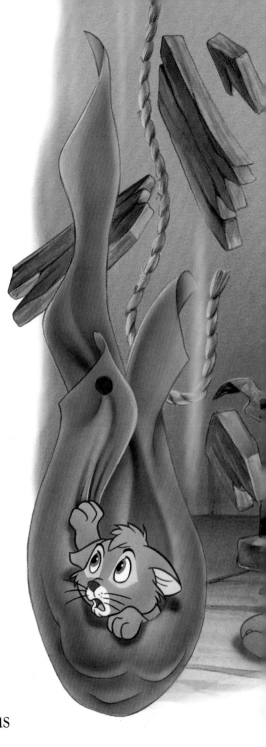

A car horn sounded outside. "I'll be right there!" Fagin called out. Then he trudged up to see Sykes, the man in the car. Fagin owed him money, but did not have a way to repay it.

While Fagin begged for more time, Sykes's dogs—a nasty pair of Dobermans—came aboard the barge and tried to frighten Dodger and his gang. When the snarling Dobermans tried to corner the kitten, he reached out and scratched one of them on the nose.

Fagin and the rest of the group were very impressed with the kitten's bravery and decided he could be part of their gang. After the day's excitement, everyone was tired. Fagin walked over to a chair, put his feet up on a footrest, and pulled out a book. While the dogs surrounded him, the kitten curled up in Fagin's lap and purred. He had found what he was looking for— a new home *and* new friends.

The next morning, Fagin was in a much better mood. He decided to take the gang into the city to get some money to pay Sykes. Dodger explained the plan to the kitten: while Tito snuck inside a parked limousine to try and steal the stereo, Einstein and Francis would distract the driver. The kitten would sit in the front seat of the car and be the lookout.

Everything was going according to plan, when—*zap!* Tito, who had been fiddling with the radio wires in the car, got an electric shock and set the alarm off! He and the gang fled as quickly as they could, but they left the kitten behind!

The kitten wasn't alone, though. A little girl named Jenny had been sitting in the backseat. "Oh, you poor kitty!" Jenny cried, when she saw how scared the kitten looked. Holding him tightly, she told the driver to take them home.

286

At home, Jenny prepared a huge bowl of food for the kitten and told him his new name was Oliver. Then she gave him a special collar and a gold identification tag. Oliver had never been happier.

Meanwhile, back at the barge, Dodger and the gang were worried about their friend. The next day, they snuck into Oliver's new house while he was sleeping and took him back to the barge. But when he woke up, Oliver was sad. He had liked spending time with Jenny.

Fagin, however, was not sad. Oliver's fancy collar and Fifth Avenue address made his eyes light up. "So that's where you've been!" he exclaimed. Fifth Avenue was where all the rich people lived. It was a jackpot! Fagin decided to contact the family, tell them that he had their cat, and ask for money. Then he could pay Sykes back.

Surrounded by his dogs, Fagin sat down and wrote a ransom letter. Then he waited for Oliver's new owners to show up. But Jenny got the note instead. When she saw that her kitten had been catnapped, she was very upset. She crept out of her house and went to save Oliver.

At the dock, she soon found Fagin. "Excuse me," she said, holding out a piggy bank filled with change. "I came to find my kitty. Somebody stole him." Fagin felt guilty about taking money from a little girl, so he gave Oliver back to her for free.

But Sykes had been following Fagin. When he saw Jenny, he knew that her parents would pay a lot of money to get her back. He grabbed the girl, pulled her into his car, and sped away.

Dodger and the rest of the gang had been waiting in the barge. They heard the commotion and rushed outside. Oliver looked miserable. "Don't worry," Dodger told him. "We'll get her back." Everyone agreed, and they ran toward Sykes's warehouse.

When the dogs arrived, Sykes was on the phone. They quietly went inside, found Jenny, and untied her. Now they all had to get away without being noticed. But it was too late! Sykes and his Dobermans had spotted them. Running as fast as they could, Dodger and the gang slid down a ramp that led outside.

Fagin was waiting for them with his scooter. Jenny and the rest of the gang jumped aboard, as Sykes and his dogs followed in their car. The chase was on! Trying to lose Sykes, Fagin drove his scooter onto the subway tracks.

The two vehicles bumped into one another, causing Jenny to be tossed around on the back of Fagin's scooter. Suddenly, she was thrown straight at Sykes. "Help!" she cried as the evil man pulled her inside his car.

Oliver jumped into the car and bit Sykes, who let Jenny go. Fagin reached behind him and pulled her back onto the scooter.

Now Oliver was in trouble. Sykes threw the kitten into the backseat and ordered his dogs to attack. Luckily, Dodger came to the rescue. Together, the pair fought off the mean dogs and jumped safely from the speeding car . . . right before it went flying off a bridge!

Jenny was overjoyed that Oliver was okay. She was never going to let anything happen to him, or his friends, ever again. Oliver purred—he felt the same way.

The very next day, Jenny had a big birthday party at her house. Fagin and the gang were all there, and they promised to visit Oliver all the time. And Jenny told them that treats would always be waiting for them. The little orphan kitten was very happy. He had finally found a home . . . and many good friends!

Long ago, in a faraway land called Agrabah, there lived a poor orphan named Aladdin. One day in the market, he stole some bread for his dinner. The Sultan's guards chased him, but he and his pet monkey, Abu, escaped. Just as Aladdin was about to eat, he noticed two children who looked hungrier than he was, so he gave the bread to them. "Things will change," he promised Abu. "Someday we'll be rich and never have any problems at all!"

That afternoon at the palace, the Sultan reminded his daughter, Princess Jasmine, that the laws of the kingdom stated she must marry a prince before her next birthday. She had just three days left. She hadn't liked any of the suitors who had proposed to her. They had only been interested in wealth and power.

Jasmine decided she would rather leave the palace than marry someone she didn't love. She disguised herself in an old peasant robe and said good-bye to her pet tiger, Rajah.

Soon, Jasmine arrived at the market. She took an apple and gave it to a child who had no money. When Jasmine could not pay for the fruit, the angry merchant called the guards. Aladdin came to her rescue and the two escaped.

When Aladdin and Jasmine were far enough away, they stopped and talked about their lives. They realized they had a lot in common.

Suddenly the guards found them. They released the princess but took Aladdin to the Sultan's dungeon. Aladdin realized he had fallen in love with Jasmine even before the guards had revealed she was a princess. But he knew she would never love him in return, for he was very poor.

Meanwhile, the Sultan's evil adviser, Jafar, had heard of a special lamp—one that would give him great power. The lamp was in the Cave of Wonders. According to legend, only a person who was a diamond in the rough could enter the Cave and come out alive. Jafar knew Aladdin had rescued the princess and thought he would be able to retrieve the lamp. He could also see how much the young man liked Jasmine.

Jafar disguised himself as an old prisoner and went into the dungeon. "Help me," he said to Aladdin. "There is a cave filled with treasure, enough to impress even your princess." In exchange, all Jafar wanted was for Aladdin to bring him the lamp. Aladdin agreed, and Jafar showed him how to escape.

Aladdin and Abu went into the Cave. A flying carpet appeared and led them to the lamp. As Aladdin reached for it, Abu grabbed a large, sparkling jewel.

The Cave began to collapse and the opening closed up. Aladdin and Abu were safe, but trapped.

"This lamp looks worthless," Aladdin said. He rubbed the dusty lamp and an enormous genie appeared.

"Master," the Genie said, "I can grant you three wishes."

Aladdin tricked the Genie into getting them out of the Cave. Then he used his first wish to become a prince so Jasmine would want to marry him. He promised to use his last wish to set the Genie free.

Later that day, Aladdin arrived at the palace in grand style, introducing himself as Prince Ali Ababwa. But Jasmine was not impressed. That evening Aladdin, as Prince Ali, invited her for a ride on the Magic Carpet. Jasmine thought that the prince looked very familiar. "You remind me of someone I met in the marketplace," she said.

"I have servants who go to the marketplace," Aladdin lied. "So, it couldn't have been me you met." But when Jasmine took his hand to step aboard the carpet, she knew she could trust him.

The Magic Carpet took them on a tour of the city and beyond, then back to the palace. "That was just wonderful," Jasmine said with a sigh. Somewhere along the way she had fallen in love.

Aladdin was thrilled that things finally seemed to be going his way.

But just then, the Sultan's guards appeared and seized the young man. Under orders from Jafar, they tossed him into the sea. Aladdin summoned the Genie and used his second wish to save his own life.

Aladdin returned to the palace to confront Jafar and reveal his true identity to the princess. Before he got a chance, Iago, Jafar's parrot, stole the magic lamp and Jafar became the Genie's new master.

"I wish to rule on high as sultan!" Jafar commanded.

The Genie was forced to obey. He lifted the palace out of the ground and placed it atop a mountain.

"You will bow to me!" Jafar ordered the princess and her father. Jasmine refused. So Jafar used his second wish to become the world's most powerful sorcerer.

Jafar changed Aladdin back into a beggar and sent him far away to a snowy wasteland. Aladdin knew he had to defeat Jafar. Luckily, he found the Magic Carpet buried in the snow, and they quickly flew back to Agrabah.

Jafar was furious when Aladdin returned. He put Jasmine inside an hourglass that was filling with sand.

Then he trapped Aladdin in a ring of
swords. But the young man pulled one
of the swords from the ground and
challenged Jafar, who transformed
into a giant snake.

Aladdin fought to free Jasmine,
but Jafar caught him in his snake coils.

"Without the Genie, boy," the evil man hissed, "you're nothing!"

Aladdin thought of a way to trick Jafar. "The Genie has
more power than you'll ever have!" he cried.

So Jafar used his third wish to become a genie. But he forgot
that genies can only come out of their lamps to serve others.
Jafar soon disappeared into a glowing black lamp.

Aladdin broke the hourglass and caught Jasmine in his arms
just before the sand completely covered her. Then, the Genie
threw Jafar's lamp far away.

Aladdin still had one wish left. Instead of asking to become a prince again, he wished for the Genie's freedom. Then he told Jasmine who he really was.

The Sultan decided to change the law so that the princess could marry whom ever she thought was worthy.

Jasmine ran into Aladdin's arms. "I choose you, Aladdin," she said tenderly. And they lived happily ever after.

Long ago, there lived a man named Geppetto who carved music boxes and clocks. One day, he made a special puppet and named it Pinocchio. That night, Geppetto saw a star in the sky and made a wish. Then he turned to his cat, Figaro, and told him, "I wished that my little Pinocchio might be a real boy!"

After Geppetto had gone to sleep, the Blue Fairy came to his workshop. "Good Geppetto," she said, "you give so much happiness to others—you deserve to have your wish come true."

The Blue Fairy touched the puppet gently with her wand. "Little puppet made of pine, wake! The gift of life be thine!" And in the blink of an eye, Pinocchio came to life.

"I can walk!" he cried. "Am I a real boy?"

"No, Pinocchio," the Blue Fairy replied. "To make Geppetto's wish come true will be entirely up to you. Prove yourself brave, truthful, and unselfish, and someday you will be a real boy."

The Blue Fairy decided to ask Jiminy Cricket to help Pinocchio. Jiminy Cricket was a small cricket who traveled from house to house looking for a warm place to stay and sing. He wore a suit and carried an umbrella. And that night, he was staying in Geppetto's workshop.

The Blue Fairy touched Jiminy Cricket with her magic wand. With that, he became Pinocchio's conscience, a voice of reason that would help the puppet know right from wrong.

As the Blue Fairy left, she said, "Now remember, Pinocchio, be a good boy and always let your conscience be your guide."

Later that night, Geppetto awoke to find his precious wooden puppet alive. He grabbed Pinocchio and swung him in the air. "It's my wish! It's come true!" he cried.

He proudly introduced his little wooden boy to Figaro and to his goldfish, Cleo. After some celebrating, they all went back to sleep.

The next morning, Geppetto gave Pinocchio an apple and a book and sent him to school. "Good-bye, son!" he called. "Hurry back!"

Pinocchio set off without Jiminy Cricket, who had overslept. Along the way, a fox named Honest John asked Pinocchio to be in a show at the theater. The fox told him he would be famous and didn't need to go to school.

Jiminy caught up with Pinocchio and tried to stop him, but the puppet had already decided to be in the show.

313

That night, Pinocchio had great fun as he danced on the stage. The audience loved him, and Stromboli, the man who put on the show, was very excited. But when Pinocchio tried to go home, Stromboli locked him in a cage.

Jiminy Cricket tried to open the cage, but he couldn't. Pinocchio began to sob. "I guess I'll never see my father again," he said sadly.

Then, the Blue Fairy appeared. She asked Pinocchio why he hadn't gone to school. He lied and told her he had met some monsters. Suddenly, his nose began to grow. Every time he lied, his nose grew a little longer! It grew so long, leaves began to grow on it, like they would on a tree branch. Finally, a nest with some birds appeared on the end of it.

"Perhaps you haven't been telling the truth," the Blue Fairy remarked. "You see, Pinocchio, a lie keeps growing and growing until it's as plain as the nose on your face."

Pinocchio promised the Blue Fairy that he would never lie again. She returned his nose to its normal size and unlocked the cage. Pinocchio and Jiminy Cricket got away from there as quickly as they could.

Pinocchio was on his way home when he ran into Honest John again. The evil fox convinced him to go to a place called Pleasure Island. So Pinocchio jumped aboard a coach with a bunch of other boys.

"Don't go, Pinoke!" cried Jiminy Cricket, but it was too late.

On Pleasure Island, Pinocchio and the other boys ran wild and stuffed themselves with sweets. Jiminy tried to get him to leave so that he'd have a chance at becoming a real boy, but Pinocchio wanted to stay. His fun did not last long, though. He suddenly began to grow donkey ears and a tail!

Pinocchio was frightened. He and Jiminy Cricket ran for their lives, away from Pleasure Island. Pinocchio wanted to go see his father.

But when they got home, Geppetto was not there. Pinocchio was very upset and wondered where his father could be. Then a dove appeared with a note. It said that Geppetto had gone to sea to look for Pinocchio. His boat had been swallowed by a whale but he was still alive.

Pinocchio set off at once to look for his father. He dove into the ocean and found him in the belly of a great whale. Geppetto was thrilled to see his son, but he didn't know how they would escape.

Then, Pinocchio had an idea—they would make the whale sneeze. Together, he and Geppetto built a fire. There was so much smoke that soon—*Ahhhhchooo!*—the whale sneezed. Father and son were thrown into the sea. Fighting the waves, Pinocchio got his father safely to shore. But the puppet was tired, and Geppetto later found him facedown in the water.

He scooped Pinocchio up and carried him home. Geppetto thought his son was gone forever. He began to cry.

But the Blue Fairy had seen how brave and unselfish Pinocchio had been, so she turned him into a boy.

Pinocchio opened his eyes and sat up. "I'm a real boy!" he cried, and hugged his father. At last, Geppetto's wish had come true, and father and son lived happily ever after.

Now the most popular Disney Storybooks have a new look!

200 Stickers Inside!

Disney
Storybook Collection
A Treasury of Tales

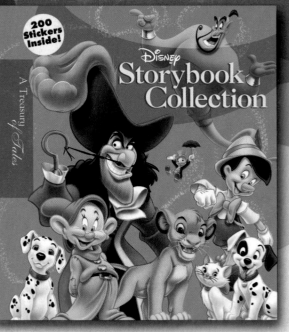

Disney PRINCESS
Princess Collection
A Treasury of Tales

200 Stickers Inside!

Disney
FRIENDSHIP STORIES
A Treasury of Tales

Including characters from your favorite Disney·PIXAR films

200 Stickers Inside!

Disney·PIXAR
STORYBOOK COLLECTION
A Treasury of Tales

200 Stickers Inside!

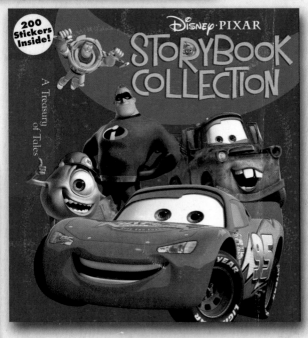

200 Stickers in Each Book!